To Howard—
Hannukah '2000
Linda

GOLFERS

Jerry Rice

SAN FRANCISCO 49ERS WIDE RECEIVER
STANFORD UNIVERSITY, GOLF COURSE
STANFORD, CALIFORNIA

"I am so addicted to golf right now, I could basically go out and play it every day."

Don't talk to Jerry Rice about going out, relaxing, and having a little fun on the golf course.

"Forget that," says Jerry. "It's not like that with athletes. It's because we're so competitive, always wanting to do it perfectly, and this is one game you're not going to master. It's very frustrating."

Golf has been frustrating Jerry for about 12 years now – every since his trainer pulled out a set of clubs and suggested that they go hit a few balls. "No problem, I thought – I'll just hit that little golf ball. I couldn't do it. I've been after it ever since."

Jerry just wishes he had started a little earlier. "I've been playing catch-up," he says. "This is a game you need to start as a kid." In fact, he adds, it's a game all kids should start playing: "I highly recommend it because it teaches such a good work ethic. Becoming a good golfer is not something that'll happen overnight. You've got to pay your dues."

The other great lesson golf teaches, according to Jerry, is to accept responsibility. "This is one game where you cannot blame anyone else," he says. "If you go out there and play bad, it's all on you."

Jerry laughs about the time he first met Tiger Woods. He had just taken up the game and Tiger came up to him on the driving range. "He says, 'Hi, Jer, how're you doing?' Then he asks me if I want to go out and play with him. I mean, my knees just buckled. There was no way I could go out there and torture Tiger that way."

Now Jerry plays to a 7-handicap and says that playing with Tiger would be "a dream come true." If the opportunity comes again, he'll definitely take it. "I've improved enough to where I think I'd be able to hit it straight."

Foster Friess

Founder of the brandywine mutual fund
Teton Pines Golf Course
Jackson, Wyoming

"I'm a scratch golfer, trapped in a 12-handicapper's body."

"I agree with the guy who said that sex is the greatest thing in the world . . . unless you're really hitting the ball."

Listening to Foster Freiss will almost convince you that there really are good reasons to play golf. He'll tell you, for instance, that golf can teach you how to deal with adversity, how to overcome mistakes rather than being "immobilized" by them. When he hits his tee-shot into the woods, instead of slamming his driver into the tee-box, he thinks about how his par is going to be so much more spectacular now than if he had hit it straight down the middle. Or if a bad shot evokes the spectre of negativity, he'll counter with "an instant balance sheet" of his life: "I'll put my loving wife, my four great kids, my nice job, my challenge, my friends on one side of the ledger, and this lousy shot on the other, and suddenly I can walk up to it with a little more enthusiasm."

He'll tell you that golf can be an important source of gratification; it can fill a need for self-improvement. "People might feel stuck in other areas of their lives," he explains. "Maybe they feel at a dead-end in their jobs, in their relationships. Golf offers the chance - the hope, anyway - of each day getting better. Sometimes you need that psychologically."

He'll tell you that golf will put you in the company of wise philosophers. "I now know," he says, "the difference between perfectionism and excellence. Perfectionism abhors error and tries to eradicate it. Excellence embraces error, builds on it, transforms it." The application to golf is self-evident. "As for me," he says, "I'm a recovering perfectionist."

Golf will certainly, Freiss will tell you, introduce you to a full rainbow of colorful characters. Like, for instance, Rocky Carbone, the caddy at Pine Valley with his own business card reading "Wind and Yardage Consultant." One day Rocky (according to Freiss's favorite story) was caddying for a man who was becoming increasingly frustrated at Pine Valley's treacherous layout - to the point that, after yet one more errant shot, he heaved his six-iron into the woods. Rocky pulled out another iron and said, "You'd better throw a provisional, sir. I doubt if we'll find that one."

And of course golf will take you to some of the earth's most beautiful places, create indelible memories, inspire priceless camaraderie, provide spellbinding stories for even the most reluctant raconteur.

Foster Freiss will tell you these things. But then, Foster Freiss has had a 34 on the back nine at Augusta.

Jay Morrish and Greg Graham

GOLF COURSE ARCHITECT AND GOLF COURSE CONSTRUCTION MANAGER
THE STONE CANYON CLUB
TUCSON, ARIZONA

"If you want to know what a person is really all about, play golf with him four or five times." (Jay Morrish)

Jay Morrish says he got into golf course architecture because he couldn't play well enough to beat anybody, but still loved the game so much he wanted to be a part of it.

He wrote to a number of prominent golf course designers, and one of the very few who responded was Robert Trent Jones Sr. "Mr. Jones told me to go back to school and get a degree in landscape architecture. I already had three and a half years of college, but I went back for another three, and when I finished up I called him. My first job was construction superintendent at Spyglass Hill."

Jay has now been in the business for thirty-six years, eleven of them working with Jack Nicklaus, whose exacting standards left an impression. "Jack wanted his tees absolutely dead level. I would try to put a 0.5 percent grade in there so that the tee would drain, and Jack would walk onto the tee, plant his feet, and say, 'No, this thing's tipping.' His feet were that sensitive."

Not that Jay and Jack didn't have "fundamental disagreements" on what makes a good golf hole. "It would be very boring if we all had the same ideas," he says, 'It's good that we're all 100 percent convinced that we're right and everybody else is wrong.'

Describing his design of Stone Canyon, Jay gives most of the credit to Mother Nature. He and Greg Graham, his construction manager, "are just the caretakers of the site," he says. At the same time, Jay is hoping for a high rating from the panelists at Golf Digest. "I don't mean to be patting myself on the back. There are a lot of architects who could have put a Golf Course of the Year on this site. We just happen to be the lucky ones who got our hands on it."

Greg agrees enthusiastically. "This was a special place – sacred ground. We just had to be sure we didn't mess it up. I mean, this is the Sistine Chapel of the desert."

Both men agree that Stone Canyon is a challenging course, but both are adamant that a good golf course is one that even a high handicapper can enjoy. "Jay and I both wanted to build a golf course that's great but where the guy that pays the freight can also play. The key to this one", says Greg, is that "Jay designed about five tees for every hole. All the rock outcroppings allowed us to do that, and they're spectacular, even if they're a hundred yards shorter than the back tees." For Jay, "the opportunity to build a course on a site like this, in my field, is like winning an Oscar."

Greg credits Arnold Palmer with articulating the fundamental concept of golf course design: "I was doing a job in Angel Park when Arnold told me, 'Never let the golf course beat the player. Always let the player beat himself.'"

Andrew Mutch

CURATOR, USGA MUSEUM
FAR HILLS, NEW JERSEY

"Everything old is new again. Take the Wilson gooseneck irons that came out in the '70s. Actually, gooseneck irons were developed in the 1890s. We just rehash the past."

You want to talk golf? Sit down with Andrew Mutch.

As a player since the age of five, he knows the feeling of hitting it flush. But as curator of the USGA Museum, he knows a lot more than that.

He knows, for instance, that the first written reference to the game came in 1457 in the Scottish Acts of Parliament. It seems that the king was trying to enact legislation demanding that his subjects forego golf in favor of sports like archery that could contribute to the national defense. "You have to figure," says Andrew, "that if the king was trying to legislate against it, the game must have already become pretty popular by the middle of the fifteenth century."

With a masters degree in illustration and some experience during graduate school working as a "glorified messenger" at the Metropolitan Museum of Art, Andrew answered a want ad in the paper for a USGA museum assistant. "I figured that working for the USGA, I'd be playing golf every day," he says. "Of course, nothing could be further from the truth."

Not that he has any regrets. In fact, he was pretty sure he had made the right career move when, six months into the job, the USGA began preparations for a Ben Hogan exhibit. "The farthest west I'd ever been was probably West Orange, New Jersey," Andrew recalls, "and here I am down in Ft. Worth walking in the front door of the Colonial Golf Club and there's Ben Hogan!" At one point during their packing of Hogan's memorabilia, says Andrew, when they were wrapping up his U.S. Open medals, Hogan leaned over one of the guys and said, "Be careful with those, son; they're hard to come by."

Subsequently, the USGA has exhibited – and Andrew has had the opportunity to get to know – most of golf's living legends: Nelson, Sarazen, Snead, Palmer, Nicklaus. Two things they had in common, according to Andrew. First was attention to detail, absolute focus. And the second? "They all had wonderful and supportive wives. If I was going to give advice to the aspiring greats of today, I'd remind them that choosing their wife is the most important decision they are ever going to make."

His work as the curator of the most extensive public collection of golf memorabilia in the world has put Andrew in a unique position – and a richly rewarding one. "Last year, for example," he says, "we had all of Walter Travis's writings donated to us. Imagine – to have a piece of golf history just dropped in your lap without any solicitation. It's such a blessing."

Arnold Palmer

"Of all the things my father taught me, the most important lesson was to treat everyone else like you'd want to be treated if you were at the other end of the line. How can you beat that? If you could get people to practice that, wouldn't we have a wonderful world."

Arnold Palmer has done it all in golf: 92 championships worldwide, including 61 on the PGA Tour; seven "major" championships, including four at the Masters and the unforgettable victory in the 1960 U.S. Open, when he came from seven strokes back in the final round; captain of the victorious 1963 Ryder Cup team; the Associated Press's "Athlete of the Decade" for the 1960s.

But it is universally acknowledged that Arnold's millions of fans around the world have been captivated by more than a golfing resume. His remarkable charisma, unfailing kindness and generosity, and down-to-earth demeanor – along with his lionhearted combativeness on the golf course – these qualities together have inspired the fanatical loyalty of "Arnie's Army."

If Arnold has had a hand in the surge in golf's popularity over the past half-century, he has a simple explanation: "I think people have seen how much I've enjoyed the game and my relationship with the game. That entices them. They just want to see if they can have as much fun as I've had."

Arnold's magnetism – and his impact on the game – are both illustrated when he mentions that he recently gave a speech to a convention of truck drivers. "I talked to them about driving trucks," says Arnold. "I told them I know how to drive an 18-wheeler, and they made me a member of their association." Not that there would have been any difficulty reaching them anyway: "The marvelous thing was that 80 percent of them played golf. Truck drivers!"

Who among these legions of new golfers might become a great champion is difficult to tell, says Arnold. "You can't always know what's in a man's heart, and that's where it comes from."

But Arnold maintains that the people who have achieved greatness carry it with them as a visible presence: "When a Doak Walker came up, you knew there was something special there. Or a Dan Marino – when he walks on the field, you know. You see it in their face, in their manner."

How about an Arnold Palmer?

Gary McCord

CBS Golf Analyst and Senior PGA Tour Player
TPC at Scottsdale
Scottsdale, Arizona

The irrepressible Gary McCord – former PGA Tour player, current Senior Tour player, veteran CBS golf analyst, author of **Just a Range Ball in a Box of Titleists,** *and world's foremost golf character.*

Never at a loss for words, Gary has a thousand explanations for golf's irresistible appeal. For instance, there's the history of the game: "the Old Course at St. Andrews . . . small-headed wooden drivers . . . stories of fleeting greatness. . . ."

Or there's golf's sensual magic: "fresh mown grass verified by early-morning dew . . . shiny new balls in your shag bag . . . the sound of new spikes crunching everything beneath them . . . the feel of a new glove stretched over your fingers . . . a light carry-bag on a spring day . . . cashmere sweaters . . . the sun setting on the 17th hole at Pebble Beach . . . squinting to see the pin on the opening hole in the day's first light. . . ."

Or the pleasure/pain of the game itself: "hitting a shot you never thought you could . . . the demons that rush through your head at the worst possible moment . . . a windy day when you're playing well and a calm day when you're not . . . taking one hole at a time and quieting the mind . . . a well-struck shot that seems stuck in the air . . . the pursuit of perfection and the awareness that you'll never achieve it. . . ."

Or the company you keep and the memories you make: "a foursome of friends . . . a good caddie . . . a round of manic highs and lows and good food and drink after . . . a round of golf with Bill Murray . . . memories of past rounds to guide you to sleep at night. . . ."

Or maybe it's just golf's unique, inimitable, bizarre personality: "dirt driving ranges with tilted barrels for your aiming pleasure . . . golf pencils . . . golf clothes adrift in a sea of fashion . . . three-wheeled golf carts ricocheting off dirt cart paths . . . golf umbrellas . . . that hideously white ball framed by the green grass. . . ."

Nor is Gary at a loss for classic golf stories – like the time he mooned the MetLife blimp during the 1990 World Series of Golf. It seems that during a commercial break, the blimp cameraman became fixated upon Gary trying to do some stretching exercises, and Gary got annoyed at seeing himself on the closed-circuit monitor. No sooner had he retaliated than he heard his producer screaming through the headset lying beside the monitor: "What the hell are you doing, you infantile idiot?" Though it hadn't gone out over the airwaves, Gary's "old, weathered bum" had been on full display in all 17 hospitality tents – not to mention in the Firestone clubhouse.

"Just another episode," says Gary, "in my quest to rid myself of any dignity I might have had left."

Maggie Hathaway

FOUNDING PRESIDENT, BEVERLY HILLS/HOLLYWOOD CHAPTER, NAACP
MAGGIE HATHAWAY GOLF COURSE
LOS ANGELES, CALIFORNIA

"Would you believe we couldn't get in public clubs?"

It was Maggie Hathaway's destiny to be enlisted in the cause of desegregating golf. Her future was revealed to her one day when she was watching her husband play with Joe Louis, who was the heavyweight boxing champion at that time. Louis, she remembers, teed off on a par-three hole but missed the green. "I told him, anybody could hit that green. That's not very far." The champ said, 'Let me see you do it. If you hit it, I'll buy you a set of clubs.'

"I did it," she says. "I hit a perfect grass-cutter that scooted all the way down the fairway and onto the green. That got me started, and I broke 100 within a year."

It also got her started on a path that would soon lead to a lawsuit, which she filed when she was denied membership in Club Links, a supposedly integrated organization of golf clubs suited to her increasing skill in the game. Her victory in the lawsuit ultimately brought an end to discrimination at all public golf courses in Los Angeles, and resulted also in the re-naming of one of those golf courses in her honor.

Ms. Hathaway, also the founding president of the Beverly Hills/Hollywood Chapter of the NAACP, waged another fight at Augusta National. As the golf writer for the *Los Angeles Sentinel*, she applied for a press pass to cover the Masters. "The Masters turned me down," she says. "They said they did not accept weekly papers." So she went to a local radio station, which sent the following letter to Chairman Charles Yates:

Dear Mr. Yates: Enclosed is our credentials application properly executed for our golf editor, Mrs. Maggie Hathaway, for one radio badge. You have our best wishes for a very successful tournament. Sincerely, Dell Shields, Executive VP and GM.

Thus, in 1975, did Maggie Hathaway become the first black sports reporter to cover the Masters.

According to Susan Henderson, who is currently the golf writer for the *Sentinel* and director of junior golf at the Maggie Hathaway golf course, the big effort now is to bring kids into the game, and she's delighted that "Maggie's course" has been designated a First Tee facility. "It's amazing to see these children," says Ms. Henderson. "Some of them only five or six years old, whose drivers are longer than they are. They hit that ball and you can see in their eyes their vision of that golf swing."

"But finally," she adds, "it's not about the golf. It's about being somebody. It's about self-esteem."

Saturday Scramble

Snake Hole Golf Club
Apache Junction, Arizona

"Golf's a lot like life. If you let it get to you, it gets to you. If you can laugh it off, it's a lot easier to take." *(Wayne Biehler)*

Judging from the dues – five dollars a year – you'd think Snake Hole might be a golf club for the rest of us. Actually, though, it's quite exclusive. You have to be a resident of the Countryside R.V. Park to belong. So says Wayne Biehler, president.

The dues includes all the golf you want to play, according to Wayne, "but you might be asked to work on the course a little bit now and then."

The good news there is that the course doesn't require a tremendous amount of maintenance. "Basically," says Wayne, "it's just a few open spots out in the desert where years ago somebody designed a little course. We don't have any grass, so we don't have to water. For tees, we've laid pieces of carpet down on the ground, and we hit off that. After that, we tee the ball up in the sand, on little plastic tee shaped like cups– saves a lot of wear and tear on the clubs. The greens are mortar sand that we've stabilized with a little used cooking oil. We loosen them up with rakes and level them off about once a week."

Wayne, still a Michigan resident except during the coldest months, has been wintering at Countryside since 1991, when a friend suggested the park to him. "I cranked up the mini-home and came down here, figuring I'd stay about three weeks. I stayed six. The next winter I figured on six weeks and stayed three months. I'm up to five months now."

Could it be the golf?

"Well," says Wayne, "the first year I came down here was the first time I ever played. Now I play every day – at least once, sometimes four times a day."

The companionship is the main thing for Wayne. "You make friends, meet a lot of good people – that's what it's all about. Just having a good time. Of course, it's very frustrating at times, especially out here when you hit them bad rocks."

Regular Foursome

Arnold Beebee, Mark Boyle, Ed Norby, Gene Van Wagoner
Sunbrook Golf Club
St. George, Utah

"At our age, we've traveled too far to get a bad lie." (Mark Boyle)

Retired district judge Arnold Beebee, now 78 years old, plays golf five or six times a week. Once a 2-handicapper, he's now a 16. "I used to think about beating up on people," he says. "Now it's just pay and play."

Former transportation lawyer Mark Boyle, now 80, plays only two or three times a week. A 9-handicap was as low as he ever got, he says, adding, "I don't have one anymore."

As their tee time approaches, they are joined by Ed Norby and Gene Van Wagoner. Gene is the golfing baby of the crowd; he's only been playing for thirty-three years. He's also the only one to have (almost) shot his age: a 66 two weeks before his own sixty-sixth birthday.

Relishing each other's company, these guys have figured out how to play golf for pleasure. "We're all old," says Arnold, "and the game is very casual. When they mow the driving range on Tuesdays, we hit a small bucket on the first tee. We hit till we're happy."

Not that the challenge of the game has relinquished its hold on them. "That's what keeps you coming back," says Ed. "The challenge of getting better, of doing it better than the last time."

"I have yet to shoot the perfect score," adds Gene. "Even that 66 I had wasn't perfect. Well, for me, maybe that is perfect."

These old guys seem to have figured out that, while you might take your swing seriously, you'd best not take yourself too seriously.

Mark says they're like the guys in the cartoon standing on the white tees, one of whom looks back at the blues and says, "Who hits from there?"

"Golfers," says his friend.

Jane Geddes and Gigi Fernandez

LPGA TOUR PLAYER AND RETIRED PROFESSIONAL TENNIS PLAYER
DEL MAR COUNTRY CLUB
SANTA FE, CALIFORNIA

"The problem with playing at my level is, you never know if you're going to shank it and kill somebody." (Gigi Fernandez)

"If I shoot a 64, I'm thinking about how I could have shot 63. That's what hooks everybody – you can't perfect it." (Jane Geddes)

Jane Geddes and Gigi Fernandez have played at the top of their respective sports. Jane has won eleven titles, including two majors, on the LPGA tour. Gigi has won seventeen Grand Slam doubles titles (including five U.S. Opens and four Wimbledons), along with two Olympic gold medals.

Their paths, in effect, have crossed. When Jane was a girl, she wanted to play competitive tennis. Realizing that she was too late ("At age 16, you already needed to be in Wimbledon, and I wasn't"), she turned instead to golf. Gigi, having retired from a stellar career in tennis, has now turned to golf.

"There's always hope in golf," both women agree.

They also agree on a theory as to why athletes from other sports find golf so compelling. "The thing is," says Jane, "most pro athletes don't consider golf a sport. The game looks easy to them, and they don't think of golfers as real athletes. Then they start playing and realize it's not so easy after all."

Gigi concurs: "I thought, 'Golf, please . . . they're not even running.' I mean, I can run and move my arm and hit a ball that's coming 100 miles per hour and put it back on the line. If I can do that, I can

certainly hit this stupid stationary ball."

Gigi got her comeuppance in her first tournament round. She hadn't played much beforehand and knew she was out of her element. "The anxiety I felt on the first tee I never had on the tennis court." The low point came on the par-three 17th, when she hit her ball into a greenside bunker. "I'd about had it at that point," she says. "Been starving for four and a half hours, and I'm standing over the ball thinking, '%!#★ this stupid game.' Well, I take a big old swing and . . . swishhh . . . I have completely missed the ball. Me, the supreme athlete, swung and missed."

Because of the honesty inherent in how the game is played – "no umpires, you call the rules on yourself" – Jane describes golf as "the game of life."

Coming from professional tennis, Gigi makes the same observation somewhat more dramatically: "I'm sorry, but in tennis it's 'You die, I win.' In golf, the players actually root for each other, say things like 'great shot' or 'tough luck.' Now I've learned to say those things and actually feel them."

As a result, says Gigi, "What I've gotten out of golf is that its taught me how to be nice."

Tim Finchem

COMMISSIONER, PGA TOUR
PONTE VEDRA, FLORIDA

" . . . if you learn this game, it will help you for the rest of your life."

Twelve years ago, Tim Finchem left Washington, where he had been representing the PGA tour, and came down to Ponte Vedra as the tour's VP of Business Affairs. Six years ago, he says, "They asked me to serve as the sheriff."

They have been good years for golf. "As you know, golf is growing, and there are a lot of balls in the air." Among the initiatives successfully juggled by Finchem, who is considered by most observers to wield more influence than any single individual in the golf industry, are the opening World Golf Village, inaugurating four World Championship tournaments, and launching the First Tee program.

Looking down the road, Finchem emphasizes the importance of spreading golf's message to more and more of the nation's youngsters. "Some of us," he says, "Were blessed in that our fathers played the game and made our access to golf possible – and affordable. But millions and millions of kids aren't that fortunate."

Television has brought the excitement of golf to all of American and has generated heightened interest in the game, but what's still missing for those who haven't gotten into the game itself is what Finchem calls "the life skills of the game." He wants young people to experience the "mental challenge of the game, the integrity of the game, sportsmanship, the etiquette of being on a golf course, because there are all skills that have a positive impact throughout a person's life."

This is the philosophy behind the First Tee Program, an initiative jointly sponsored by the PGA Tour, the United States Golf Association, and the Professional Golfers of America that is designed to bring golf to kids that might not otherwise have the experience. "My message to the kids is that we're coming with the First Tee to give you the opportunity to learn this game. And if you learn this game, it will help you for the rest of your life."

Rocky Carbone

Caddy
Pine Valley Golf Club
Pine Valley, New Jersey

"I always said even if I was a millionaire, I would still caddy here. I've caddied at other courses where they treat caddies like they're something stuck on the bottom of their shoe."

Rocky Carbone's story teaches the comforting lesson that, even in this confusing and frustrating world, sometimes a man and his profession are ideally matched.

"One time," says Rocky, "I was caddying for Terry Francona, manager of the Phillies. Now I'm five-feet-six, and he's maybe six-three. We're on the 17th, a short par four but it's uphill and the green sits up pretty high. So he hits his second shot from maybe 130 yards out and says, 'Rock, is that on the green?' I said, 'Terr, come here a minute.' I says, 'Scootch down a little.' He squats down a little, and I tell him to get down a little lower. He squats down a little more, and I says, 'Just a little bit lower.' Finally he gets down to where his head's about level with mine and I says, 'Now, that's what I see. How the frig do I know if it's on!'"

It's not just that Rocky loves golf, though that's a big part of it.

"On the 14th hole I had a guy once named Bubbles. The 14th, you know, goes over the lake, and I'm handing him his five-iron. He says, 'No, no, I'm gonna hit a six.' I says, 'Bubbles, hit your five.' 'No, gimme the six.' So he's about to hit and I says, 'Bubbles, wait a minute.' I leaned over to the ball and said, 'Take a deep breath, honey, you're about to go under.'"

It's not just that he loves Pine Valley, though that's certainly a huge part of it. He remembers sitting in front of the TV with his wife when Bob Hope told Barbara Walters that his favorite stop on tour was the Valley Forge Music Center "because I get to play Pine Valley." "I mean," says Rocky, "my wife's teeth just about fell out of her head. For somebody of that stature to say something like that."

For Rocky, Pine Valley has it all: beautiful architecture ("take any hole off Pine Valley and put it on any other course, and it'll be one of the best holes on that course"); atmosphere, history, and absolute respect among members, staff, and guests. And somehow all this without being "snooty." Yes, he loves golf. Yes, he loves Pine Valley. But there's one more thing.

"This guy hits his drive in the woods and asks me if he should hit another one. I say, 'Noooo! Better lookin' for one than lookin' for two.' His round is going, like, 10, 7, 9, 7, 6, 8. Finally we get to a short par 4 and he makes a five. He turns to me and goes, 'Rock, there goes my bogey-free round.'"

And it's that other thing – the exuberant, irrepressible storytelling – that gives ultimate credence to Rocky's enviable claim: "I get paid to have fun."

Gary Gilchrist (with Aree Song Wongluekiet)

DIRECTOR OF GOLF, DAVID LEADBETTER ACADEMY
BRADENTON, FLORIDA

"The biggest secret to this game, basically, is hard work. There are no short-cuts. This is what life's all about: it's not about winning the race; it's about finishing the race."

Gary Gilchrist leads by example. He loved playing golf from the age of three, when his father cut down some clubs for him to use, but he also realized early on that to get good at the game was a demanding proposition.

"The game of golf didn't come easy to me," he says, "so I know what these kids go through." He remembers the tournaments he played in as a teenager, where the young phenoms would hit their drives and then reach the green with an eight-iron. "I would hit the driver, then my three-wood, and then a nine-iron."

But the young South African persevered, and was good enough at the end of high school to win a scholarship to Texas A&M. After college he returned to play on the South African tour for five years, then returned to the U.S. to improve his game under the tutelage of David Leadbetter. Instead, he found an opportunity. The Leadbetter Academy was getting off the ground – and looking for instructors. "It fits my personality," says Gary. "For some reason, I'm more worried about somebody else's game than my own."

Certainly Gary's work ethic had found its proper home. "There's so much instruction out there," he says, "but there's not a whole lot of 'you need to train' out there." Gary admits that his staff and students "maybe take the game a little more seriously than the average person out there," but, he adds, "we're seeing some amazing results." Such as 13 year old phenom Aree Song Wongluekiet and her twin sister Naree who are ranked the number 2 and 3 junior girls in the U.S..

Gary emphasizes, though, that even those results – and the more than one hundred national titles won by his students – are not ultimately the point. His hope is that the lessons his students learn at the academy – lessons about discipline, work, responsibility, personal relationships – will last a lifetime.

"Not everybody who comes here will be a superstar," says Gary, "but we can try to help build the heart of a champion. I tell my students, 'Train, believe in yourself even when things aren't going great, face disappointment and learn how to handle it. See yourself as a champion, not just on the golf course, but in life.'"

It's a long road, as Gary sees it, "and there are no short-cuts."

Andy Mill

FORMER OLYMPIC SKIER
ADIOS GOLF CLUB
DEERFIELD BEACH, FLORIDA

". . . its almost like a religion, if you will, this game of golf."

Being a member of the U.S. Olympic Ski Team for 10 years merely constituted a brief hiatus from Andy Mill's real sport. "I started playing golf when I was seven years old," Andy says, "when we were living in Laramie, Wyoming. I'll never forget learning how to swing the club in the open fields across from our house. One day my dad was standing behind me and I whacked him on the head and gave him nine stitches. He gave the game up, but 32 years later I'm still playing."

One of the things Andy loves best about golf is "the standard of greatness" built into the game. "If you play tennis, or ski, or race a car, or fish, what's your standard for how well you did? In golf, the standard of par gives you that immediately."

Andy has been around competitive sports all his life. Married to tennis great Chris Evert, he currently hosts and produces the fishing show Sportsman's Journal. Golf is unique among sports, though, in the way that "it challenges you not only physically, but it challenges your personal integrity."

Elaborating, Andy says, "You see these guys on the tour maybe play the wrong ball or sign the wrong score card, and they disqualify themselves, which costs them thousands and thousands of dollars. But that's the name of the game. It's a game of integrity, and that's it."

As for the physical challenge, Andy has his own take on that as well. "What does it for me is not necessarily hitting the huge drive, or getting on a par-five in two, or even making the eagle. For me it's making the three-foot putt to save par. I think the real challenge of the game is in saving par. That's where your nerves are really tested. I'll always remember when President Ford said that the only thing that could make the leader of the most powerful country in the world shake was having to make a three-foot putt for par."

It's this challenge – on every level – that keeps us from walking away from the game, says Andy. "The fact is that we as human beings like to be challenged. And in golf, every shot is a challenge. Every shot."

Bill Rockwell

WORLD PUTTING CHAMPIONSHIPS COMPETITOR
TORREY PINES GOLF CLUB
SAN DIEGO, CALIFORNIA

"I beat Rocky Thompson on the practice green, but he kicked my butt in the real tournament. He really smoked me. I was thinking I was good until he came.

Bill Rockwell took an unusual route to the World Putting Championships. He had always liked golf, even as a child, and began playing when he was 14. But at the age of 19 he crashed his motorcycle into the side of a car.

"I was just being a reckless teenager," Bill says, "not paying attention and going too fast." A car pulled out in front of him and he slammed into the driver's side door. "I knocked the car sideways four feet and pushed the door in past the steering wheel. They told me I died three times and they revived me all three times, so I guess I just wasn't ready to die."

However, Bill did lose one arm and the use of the other arm in the wreck, which would seem to have brought his golfing days to an end. But a friend suggested that he could probably play miniature golf, and Bill says that got him thinking. He bought himself a putter at Kmart and figured out a way to swing it – standing on one foot, holding it between the toes of the other foot, braced behind his knee. "It just came to me like that," he says. "Boom! Just like it was meant to be. Swung it a couple of times and never changed it."

From the miniature golf course Bill quickly moved onto the putting green and within six months was putting in his first qualifying tournament. He won his club tournament and moved on to the Regionals at Torrey Pines, where he came to the attention of Dave Pelz, short game guru and director of the World Championships.

Bill placed 11th in the Regionals, which he says wasn't quite good enough to qualify for the Championships, but Pelz granted him an exemption. "Dave wanted to see me putt in that tournament for sure," says Bill. "He saw it as an inspirational thing, and he really wanted me to have the experience of competing with all those guys."

Bill didn't merely compete. He placed 158th out of the 300 best putters in the world, in the process beating out some twenty PGA tour players. He also earned a feature story in Pelz's forthcoming Putting Bible.

"It was the greatest experience," Bill says. "I had no problems out there on the green. Out there I just focused. Except when I looked at the leader board and saw my name up there. I went to the dirt after that. Oh no, I shouldn't have looked at that."

Dave Pelz

DAVID PELZ GOLF INSTITUTE
AUSTIN, TEXAS

"There is no recovery from a missed short putt."

Dave Pelz is on a mission. He's by-golly going to make you a better golfer. How? By cleansing you of the sins of your unholy short game.

"I believe there's always hope!" Dave shouts from the pulpit. And after a very few minutes in your mortifying pew in the Church of Dave, you're ready to shout back, "Amen!"

"Go ahead," says Dave to his wayward flock, "and mess up all you want to – until you get inside a hundred yards. Then it's time to tighten up. You can hit the two most God-awful shots in the world, but if you happen to hole out the third one, you've just made birdie or eagle."

Tell it, brother. Tell about salvation.

Dave, guru of the greenside, preaches his gospel in his new instructional book *The Short Game Bible*, as well as in person to all willing listeners: "You don't need to hit it long," he admonishes. "You just need to get it in the hole. That is a learned skill, not a God-given talent. This game is a great equalizer. You or I or our grandmothers can make a putt as well as Arnold Palmer or Tiger Woods or David Duval."

Such was the inspiration for Dave's World

Putting Championship, which in turn has engendered countless inspirational testimonials. "We had a ten-year-old boy out-putt Payne Stewart and a man with no arms beat twenty tour players. We had a ninety-five-year-old man who led the Champion-ship for several holes. I will never be able to dunk a basketball like Michael Jordan," declaims Dave, "but I can out-putt that son-of-a-gun every day."

Like all journeys, this one is best taken one day at a time. "I understand now that improvement is where the enjoyment comes from," says Dave. "That's why I've focused on the short game. Not only is it where people make or break their score, but it's where you can continue to get better no matter your age.

Or maybe three days at a time. "Three days that will change your game forever – that's the slogan of our school. Because when you learn how to do it, you never forget. When you learn how to hit a wedge shot, when you learn how to read a green, you know it forever."

"That's the beauty of our program," says Dave. "If you keep working at it, you can improve as long as you can walk and swing a club."

Hallelujah!

Dave Alvarez (with Bob Magoon)

PGA GOLF PROFESSIONAL
RIVER VALLEY RANCH GOLF CLUB
CARBONDALE, COLORADO

"I can't think of a better game for kids to play because eventually it will dawn on them, 'Wow, this game is bigger than I am. I've got two choices: don't play it anymore or get better.'"

Upstate New York-native Dave Alvarez has been playing golf "seriously" since he was 12 years old. As a freshman in high school, he made the varsity golf team, and by age 14 he was qualifying for the New York State Junior Championship. He has played in three U.S. Opens and two Senior U.S. Opens, and his 63 at Fisher's Island broke by two strokes the course record – set by Bobby Jones in 1936.

Dave came early to golf, but as he admits, only by staying long has he come to understand the game. "When I was younger I didn't really appreciate golf – the nuances, the history, the camaraderie, the lure of playing a game that will make you smile one day and hammer you into submission the next."

In other words, Dave says, "As I got older, I realized how hard the game was."

But with the hard lessons come rich compensations – special moments, indelible memories. Like the round Dave played with Gary Player and Bob Charles in the Senior Open at Olympia Fields: "You've got to understand, if it hadn't been for guys like Gary and Arnold Palmer, my friends and I might have ended up in reform school. I told him right to his face, 'You

know, you have no idea what you meant to us, to our idea of what the game of golf is, what it means to be a golfer.' "He says, 'I appreciate your saying that. As I get older, I appreciate all the compliments I can get.' It was great."

And then there's the satisfaction of the life well spent. Like many talented young players, Dave faced a tough decision. "There were people pushing me, wanting to sponsor me, but I never really aspired to go out on the tour. I always enjoyed the teaching side, the people, being at the club. For me, the ultimate is see-ing the pleasure people get out of the game as you're helping them get better."

Like 66-year-old retired opthamologist Bob Magoon, who started playing when he was 45, quit for ten years, and resumed at age 60. Bob calls himself "a scratch golfer on the driving range," but on the course, he says, "It's just so difficult."

With Dave's help, though, he's working at it. At the same time he's working at managing his expecta-tions: "I know I'm not going to beat it. I'm just look-ing to get respectable."

He's in good hands. After all, Dave is in his 32nd year as a teaching pro.

Joe Gibbs

PRESIDENT AND CEO, THE GOLF CHANNEL
ORLANDO, FLORIDA

"People just dream about stuff like this happening. I didn't ask for it, didn't plan it, but all of a sudden, there is this guy."

In 1988 Joe Gibbs bought a house at Shoal Creek in Birmingham, Alabama. He had just sold a cable company and planned to do a lot of traveling with his wife.

He also decided, at age 40, to take up golf. "I figured if I was going to live at Shoal Creek I ought to learn how to play the game."

When the PGA Championship came to Shoal Creek in 1990, Joe was both an enthusiastic golfer and a willing host with a guesthouse available on the tournament site. Arrangements were made for Ben and Julie Crenshaw to stay with Joe and his wife, but at the last minute – "after my wife had spent a week preparing" – the Crenshaws changed their plans.

At registration on Tuesday, tournament director Mike Thompson overheard Winnie Palmer complaining about her and Arnold's hotel accommodations. He immediately spoke up: "Well, Joe Gibbs would love to have you stay with him." Arnold headed out to play a practice round and left Winnie to go check out the accommodations at the Gibbs' guesthouse. She found them quite satisfactory.

Joe's job was to catch up with Arnold on the golf course and tell him of the new arrangement. As Joe remembers it, "Arnold, his caddy, and I were the last threesome to walk the back nine that afternoon – us

and the 3,000 spectators following Arnold's every step." Watching Arnold work that crowd – talking, joking, laughing – gave Joe a close encounter with the fabled Palmer charisma. "I was just in awe," he says.

The Palmers stayed with the Gibbses for the next four days, and, says Joe, "We just became friends." The Palmers returned the hospitality a couple of months later, hosting Joe and his wife for a weekend in Orlando.

"Six months later I got the idea," says Joe. "I had fallen in love with golf, had become friends with Arnold, and had been reading about how niche programming on cable was the wave of the future. I asked myself, what are people going to want to watch that they don't have today?'"

Joe did a little polling, then called Arnold, who quickly flew to Birmingham. Arnold was interested enough to pick up the phone and call Mark McCormack at IMG. Once IMG had formulated a business plan that looked promising, says Joe, "Arnold came in as my partner and reimbursed me half of everything I'd put in up to that point. We became co-founders and started raising money, and here we are."

Where, exactly, is here? "Well," says Joe, "we have about 30 million subscribers worldwide right now, and we're adding about seven million subscribers a year. We've done very well."

Gary and Jack Nicklaus

Doral Ryder Open
Miami, Florida

"Golf is an endless quest. Just when you think you've got the game solved, it presents another mystery. The same sport that intrigued and challenged me at age ten does the same for me at age sixty." (Jack Nicklaus)

"Nobody masters this game," says Jack Nicklaus. If anybody has the authority to make this pronouncement, it's Jack, the man who came closest.

Jack Nicklaus, winner of one hundred tournaments worldwide, including a record-never-to-be-approached twenty major championships, was honored by his peers in 1999 as the Golfer of the Century. His observations carry weight.

"Golf has such a powerful hold on us," he declares "because it is so difficult to play well. And because no matter how well you play, you still haven't mastered the game. Everybody comes back for more. No matter who you are or how old you are or how good you think you are, golf challenges you to get even better."

Golf isn't just difficult; it flaunts its difficulty. As Jack says, "To quote Mr. Churchill, 'Golf is a game that consists of getting a small ball into an even smaller hole with implements singularly ill-designed for the purpose.'" The fact that we still insist on playing it, says Jack, suggests that it's "a pretty special game."

Having lived one of golf's exemplary lives, Jack is quick to credit golf for the values it embodies and lessons it teaches: "Golf teaches you patience; it teaches you discipline; it teaches you humility; it teaches you how to get along with other people; it teaches you sportsmanship; it teaches you how to handle success and how to handle failure.

But mostly, says Jack's son Gary, as he relishes his first full season on the PGA Tour, golf teaches you patience. "I learned about patience as a junior golfer, then at the collegiate level. In each of the nine times I tried to qualify for the PGA Tour, I learned another lesson about patience. And in every event I play, I am taught new lessons in patience."

Gary considers himself very fortunate to have grown up in a golfing family without having had the game forced down his throat. "My father always offered his support, but he never pushed," says Gary. And being allowed to learn the game on his own terms meant that he could truly enjoy golf for all that it offers – the beauty of the outdoors, the ultimate mental challenge, the bond with his family.

Jack, in turn, says he's extremely proud of what Gary has achieved to make it onto the tour. "I watch and admire all his hard work," says Jack. "I only wish for him to have success and enjoy some of the things that have made my life so full."

Spoken like a champion – and a dad.

Bob (Doc) Graves

GOLF COURSE MEASURER
ARIZONA

"I like to look at the flowers, the trees, I like to watch the grass grow."

After twenty-five years as a chiropractor, "Doc" Graves decided it was time for an adjustment. He gave up his day job and now works eighty hours a week for the Arizona Golf Association.

In addition to being on the association's board of directors, he is also on the Rating Team – in which capacity he has measured, and played, every golf course in the state of Arizona.

That may help to explain the hip replacement surgery, which, along with the arthritis in his feet and neck, have reduced him to having to use a golf cart. "If I could still walk," he says wistfully, "I'd still be playing that scratch golf. I haven't had a 71 since the surgery."

A player since the age of 13, a tournament competitor since 16, and now a devoted golf official, Doc has seen it all: "I once saw my ball disappear into a hole that two minutes earlier I'd seen a rattlesnake crawl into. When I looked into the hole, I didn't see the ball or the snake. I've seen power lines down on a golf course, swarms of bees, clubs hurled in anger. I saw a guy throw a club one time and it broke and the shaft sunk into this other guy's leg, right into the femoral artery. It almost killed him."

Doc has no patience with such behavior. In fact, he has little sympathy with overcharged intensity that so many people bring to the golf course. "I've played with people who didn't realize they had roses behind the first hole. People who can play a whole round without seeing anything beautiful on the course. I don't know why that is."

For Doc, being in the out of doors is a big part of the pleasure of golf: "I like to look at the flowers," he says, "the trees . . . I like to watch the grass grow." Not surprisingly, he has become interested in golf's environmental issues, the use of pesticides and herbicides, and he talks animatedly about the new kind of hazard – "environmentally sensitive areas" – beginning to show up on golf courses: "You see a hazard marker with green on top of the stick, it means you can not enter that area. That's sacred ground. Keep out!"

If respect for nature's beauty is one of the virtues that golf helps to instill, respect for the rules of the game is another – especially, perhaps, from the perspective of an official. "The fundamental thing that I have learned," says Doc, "is that golf is a gentleman's game. Be honest. Don't move the ball. The game has increased my own integrity."

Doc shakes his head. "Believe me, I've seen them cheat in funny ways. Who are they kidding?" Because, as Doc says and as golfers universally agree, one of the abiding allurements of the game is that "it's completely individual" – every man against himself.

Jim Kidd (with Gus)

DIRECTOR OF GOLF
SAND HILLS GOLF CLUB
MULLEN, NEBRASKA

"It's hard to explain, but there's some sort of addiction there. It's like a drug. Once it gets in your system, it's hard to get out. Golfers know."

If anybody was ever to the fairway born, it's Jim Kidd. His grandfather, a club champion in Scotland, came to America in 1905 with the ambition of becoming an engineer. But those plans were derailed, and by 1920 he had become the head pro at the renowned Interlochen Country Club in Minneapolis in 1920, a post he held until 1957. What's more, Jim's father then took over and remained Interlochen's head pro until 1993.

As for Jim, his grandfather gave him his first set of clubs when he was four, he won his state high school championship, and he earned All-America honors in college. He tried briefly to dodge his fate, but five years in commercial real estate were sufficient to remind him where his heart, mind, soul, and body belonged.

Like a primordial urge, his bloodline led him to his present position at Sand Hills, a Ben Crenshaw/Bill Coore design that he believes is as close to Scotland as you can find in the U.S. "For Ben and Bill, the land dictated the flow of the holes, just like it does in Scotland. They didn't have to move a lot of earth – just followed nature." And as it is to so many golfers, the sense of being in the natural world is of paramount importance to Jim. "To be able to stand on a tee box and look out for miles and miles and not see anything made by man is incredible."

Of the people interviewing for the Sand Hills job, Jim recalls, he was the only one who actually went out and walked the course. Clearly, it wasn't a good walk spoiled. He immediately called his wife and said, "This is it; this is where I want to be."

Consider the man fortunate whose heritage, desires, and abilities all lead him to the same spot. How many U.S. club pros can go to a tradition-steeped course in Scotland and find their grandfather's name listed on the Champion's Board for 1903 and 1904? "I really think that in choosing to be here at Sand Hills," says Jim, "I'm as close to the golf world that my grandfather and his friends knew as I'm likely to get here in America."

Jim gives the design team a lot of credit for the feel of this course that he loves, just as he also credits Crenshaw and Coore for one of his favorite golfing memories: "We all just had a small bag – Sunday bags – and we just went out and walked and played golf. Between the three of us there were maybe five words said the whole time. We were like little kids again, just playing golf. Ben said that was one of the funnest times he had had on a golf course in a long time. I had to agree."

Bill Coore and Ben Crenshaw

GOLF COURSE DESIGNERS
CHECHESSEE GOLF CLUB
BLUFFTON, SOUTH CAROLINA

"When played on courses constructed in harmony with nature, golf becomes a connection to the natural world."

Bill Coore might well have ended up designing foreign language curricula on a college campus. With a major in classical Greek from Wake Forest, Bill was headed to graduate school at Duke when the draft board intervened in 1969. After his two-year hitch in the army, he says, "I just couldn't get back in the school mode."

Instead, he started watching a golf course under construction near his mother's house in North Carolina, being built by "some guy nobody had ever heard of – Pete Dye." Bill says he was fascinated by what he saw, and once he managed to get hold of Dye's phone number, "I pestered him until he gave me a job. So instead of graduate school, I went to the school of Pete Dye."

In 1981, by which time he had become golf course superintendent at Waterwood National in East Texas, he was approached by some people who wanted him to design a course in the South Texas town of Rockport. "They told me I could do whatever I wanted as long as I didn't spend one penny more than they had available. So I went out there with a couple of guys, and from that golf course came our company."

Only one thing was lacking – at least in the eyes of potential clients. "People would say that nobody's ever heard of me. Why didn't I work with a well-known player?" But Bill didn't like the idea, just wasn't comfortable with it. When one prospective customer persisted, Bill mentioned that the only player he could imagine working with was Ben Crenshaw.

"The guy looks at me and says, 'Oh my God. I know Ben. He's as romantic and naïve as you are. You two would be a total disaster.'"

Wrong.

It turns out that Ben had heard about the course Bill had designed in South Texas and wanted to see it. A meeting ensued, which evolved eventually into a friendship and ultimately, by 1985, into a partnership. "At some point," Bill recalls, "we decided that we were pretty compatible philosophically and personally."

By all accounts, eloquent testimony to their successful union can be found in the renowned Sand Hills Golf Club in Mullen, Nebraska. On such a site, says Bill, "if you don't do something extraordinary, you have failed."

But Chechessee Creek, on which the team is currently at work, should also provide the kind of experience that Bill hopes players take away from his courses. "We want our players to be challenged, but not overwhelmed; we want them to be encouraged to play in a thoughtful fashion; and, if we have done our job of building the course so that it complements its natural surroundings, we want players to be inspired by the course's beauty.

"To have fun playing and leave with a sense of inspiration. I don't think you can ask for any more than that."

Norman V. Swenson, Jr.

PLAYER AND COLLECTOR
CHARLOTTE, NORTH CAROLINA

"Golf is the only sport I know where you get to spend four or five quality hours actually getting to know who your opponent is."

"I don't really play much golf except competitively," says Norman Swenson, Jr.. "I try to play only in tournaments, because that's the true measure of how you're doing. You have the score card in your hand, and you play exactly by the rules, and you putt out every putt, and your score, of course, compares to everybody else's in the tournament."

Sounds like a guy who doesn't quite grasp the concept of the mulligan.

Norman started playing golf at Carmel Country Club in Charlotte when he was a kid, immediately fell in love with the game, and never looked back. When he and his cohorts got to driving age, he says, "We'd put our headlights on the putting green and practice after dark if we had a competition coming up."

When his high school team won the state regionals, he was the medalist in the tournament. From there he went to Wake Forest, one of the premier golf programs in the country, where among his teammates was Lanny Wadkins. "It's one of my claims to fame," he says, "that I was the only amateur from that team. Everybody else turned pro."

As an amateur Norman has distinguished himself: runner-up in two North Carolina State Amateurs, runner-up in the South Carolina Amateur, semi-finalist in the Maryland Amateur. But the biggest thrill in his golfing life came recently: "I qualified for the British Senior Open at age fifty-two last year. Only six amateurs in the world made that field."

Having sold his successful business five years ago and finding himself with more time on his hands that he could fill by playing, Norman began collecting. He now has one of the finest private collections of golf memorabilia in the nation. Among his most prized items is a letter from Bobby Jones to Cyril Tolley, whom Jones beat to win the Grand Slam, in which "Jones compliments Tolley for hitting what he thought was the finest golf shot he had ever seen." Norman also has an autographed picture of Tom Morrison, the earliest golf pro, along with what is considered one of the oldest putters still in existence.

In fact, Norman's collection is so extensive and of such interest that two years ago he conceived the idea of putting together a "traveling museum." With the help of some of the PGA's corporate sponsors, he has been exhibiting a collection of his most prized items at selected PGA tour sites. "The fans go to these tournaments," he says, "but don't really know any of the history – the evolution of the golf ball, of the golf club, of the putter. It's been very gratifying to me that people can see these great golf artifacts that they'd never had an opportunity to see before."

Tom and Eri Crum

PEAK PERFORMANCE COACH AND AUTHOR OF "JOURNEY TO CENTER" (TOM)
GOLF PROFESSIOAL, ASPEN GOLF CLUB (ERI)
BOCA DEL MAR COUNTRY CLUB, BOCA RATON, FLORIDA

"Golf is the only mind/body art I know where the movement is slow enough for you to see exactly where the mind interferes with the body." (Tom Crum)

Don't take your cell phone onto the course with Tom Crum. "You can't play golf being somewhere else," says this longtime martial arts instructor and performance expert. "Being fully present is not an easy task today, in this crazy, busy world, but that's what golf asks you to do – to be fully present and in the moment."

For Tom, golf is an ideal discipline for approaching the fundamental principle of centering. "Centering is that place where the mind and body and spirit become one and you're able to literally let it happen." This is the real reason, Tom explains, why so many people define the essential pleasure of the game in terms of hitting "that one good shot." They have experienced that "place of purity where you're not doing it; it's being done to you."

If self-knowledge is the end of the quest, golf is the path. "Golf is a game of looking at who you are," says Tom. "It's a wonderful mirror to the soul. The beautiful thing is that the humbling moments are as powerful as the moments when you're in the zone. It's extraordinary to go out on the course and not just be playing the game to score, but to be playing the game of awareness."

The huge appeal of the game in Japan is no surprise to Tom. "They understand that they are exploring an art," he says. "That's why if they can't get on a course, they still hit from rooftops into nets."

Tom's son Eri played golf for Stanford with teammates Tiger Woods, Notah Begay III, and Casey Martin, among other notables. In his effort to join his former teammates on the PGA Tour, Eri has absorbed his father's teachings. "When I'm in the zone and shooting in the 60s, I sense that it's happening naturally. I'm centered, in a state of full power, my energy flowing outwardly. It's effortless."

The difference between Eri and the pros at the top of the leaderboard on Sunday, says Tom, is that they have developed the ability to "access the zone more readily."

"It's an inner game," Tom emphasizes, "at a very high level. And it's fascinating to watch the geniuses at work – to see them call it forth."

Renee Powell

CURRICULUM CONSULTANT AT THE FIRST TEE/HEAD GOLF PROFESSIONAL AT CLEAR VIEW GOLF CLUB IN OHIO
WORLD GOLF VILLAGE
ST. AUGUSTINE, FLORIDA

"In terms of who can play, golf has no restrictions. The golf ball doesn't know whether you're young or old, male or female, big or little."

In 1995, after thirteen years on the LPGA Tour, Renee Powell became head professional at Clear View Golf Club in East Canton, Ohio. Life after the tour has given her a chance to get more involved in an aspect of the game that's close to her heart.

"I have always been involved in junior golf because I grew up playing golf. My father first put a club in my hand when I was three, so I spent years in junior golf. From my own experience, I realize what the game of golf can do in building the character of young people."

Renee is now an integral part of the First Tee Program, which she sees as "the first time that all the major golf organizations have come together for the one good purpose of getting young people involved with golf."

Specifically, Renee is helping develop the First Tee curriculum, which divides the game into such areas of study as rules, etiquette, golf course care, and, of course, the fundamentals of actually playing. Kids in the program will acquire this knowledge one level at a time, and once they have advanced through all the levels of study, they'll receive certification. "They'll carry cards certifying that they can go to any course and play in a safe, fast, and courteous way," says Renee.

Renee believes that golf can teach children all of life's fundamental lessons: discipline, self-confidence, integrity, along with the ability to deal with adversity. "Golf rewards you for hitting a good shot," she says, "but you're going to hit some bad shots, too, and you have to deal with that. Just like the game of life."

Plus, on a very practical level, a serious interest in golf is just bound to keep kids out of trouble. "Golf takes time," says Renee. "You're not going to be out running the streets if you really want to become good at golf."

Beyond that, her work on behalf of junior golf gives Renee a chance to apply one of the great lessons that she learned as a child: "One thing that my parents always taught us was that you have to be sure to give back — to make the world better that it was when you found it. I feel that with junior golf and the First Tee Program, I am trying to do that."

Cecil Brandon, Jr.

FATHER OF MYRTLE BEACH HOLIDAYS
MYRTLE BEACH, SOUTH CAROLINA

"Golf is such a fabulous game. The combination of the beautiful outdoors, friends, clean fresh air – not to mention that most of us enjoy a little gambling. It's a game you can play till you die."

In 1963, Myrtle Beach Golf Holiday represented ten hotels and eight golf courses and had a budget of $43,000. Today, it represents and promotes 103 golf courses and has a budget of $5,000,000.

What happened? Two words, says Cecil Brandon Jr., who served as executive director of the organization for thirty years: free golf.

"One of our enterprising members went around to some of the golf courses and said, 'If you give us free greens fees in December and January and part of February, we'll guarantee you so much play the rest of the year.' Very smart. And as a result, the world discovered Myrtle Beach."

"Even with 103 courses available," adds Cecil, "you'd be hard pressed to find a tee time in February." The free golf may be gone, he says, "but in relation to the rest of the world, we're still the best bargain in golf." Not to mention the phenomenal weather, the fifteen hundred restaurants, and what Cecil calls "the most gorgeous beach from Maine to Florida."

But Cecil admits that you can have too much of a good thing. "I knew it was going to grow. The main thing was just to try to hold on to healthy growth, like we had for so long. Now we've got greedy growth, and you know what greed does to everything in the world."

The proliferation of up-scale courses and developments has had its effect, making it harder to identify Myrtle Beach as the "blue-collar golf capitol of the world" ("other people liked to put that onus on us," says Cecil), but the resort still draws "a cross-section of everybody." Cecil clearly enjoys the fact his visitors are "tremendously happy" to find plenty of courses to play for twenty-five or thirty dollars.

And he speaks with special animation about the Dupont World Amateur, the world's largest on-site golf tournament, which is owned by Golf Holiday. "It's a world handicap championship," Cecil says. "You want to see golfers from all walks of life? We've got CEOs, truck drivers, women, kids – it's just a real celebration of golf."

This diversity is crucial for golf's future, Cecil believes. In fact, he strongly recommends that the governing bodies of the sport give serious thought to building courses in the inner cities – nine-hole courses where kids can play for free. "We've got to get more kids playing golf," he says. "It's one of the most important things we can do. And everybody can play – girls, boys, big, little – doesn't matter. Everybody."

Brian Pavlet

PROFESSIONAL LONG DRIVER
RAVEN GOLF CLUB, PHOENIX, ARIZONA

"The thing about golf is that the bad shot you just hit is not the important one anymore. The important one is the next one."

The first time I hit a golf ball it went a long way," says Brian Pavlet, the 1993 National Long Drive Champion.

But it wasn't until he and his brother were looking for an excuse to go to Vegas that Brian entered his first competition. "There were all these guys who looked like they could play for the Cardinals, swinging 50-inch drivers and really hitting it out there. I told my brother to forget it; I wasn't going to make an idiot out of myself. He literally had to push me onto the tee box."

Brian hit it 367, and a career was born.

Winning the championship in '93 was not his biggest kick, says Brian. That came at the Phoenix Open in 1995 – "the year John Daly was it."

The Phoenix Open always had a long-drive event preceding the tournament, recalls Brian, and this year the organizers, with announcer Gary Koch, decided to have a little fun with John Daly and his fellow pros. By pre-arrangement, when Koch asked if there was anybody in the crowd who can hit with these guys, Brian raised his hand and stepped forward – even though, as he says, "Why anyone would want to hit in front of 25,000 people is beyond me."

On cue, Brian hooks his first ball. "Then Gary tells me, 'Hey, Brian, you've got a great swing. I bet if you were to line your left thumb up with your left nostril

and breathe through your eyelids you could really hit it.'"

With these "professional tips" in mind – but still secretly instructed to hold back – Brian hits a couple of balls past the 300-yard mark. At that point Koch reveals the ruse, introduces Brian, and gives him one last ball, saying, "OK, show them what you can really do."

"One ball," recalls Brian. "My heart was coming through my chest. But I teed it up and hit one of the best golf shots I have ever hit in my life. I killed it. I mean, that thing was crushed. While it was still in the air, I turned to Gary Koch and said, 'That's gonna hit the 350-sign on the fly.' And it did – hit it dead center. The crowd went nuts."

It's reassuring when such a wonderfully fun moment comes to the kind of person who knows how to fully appreciate it. "There's one thing I try to convey to the people who come to my clinics and exhibitions: we play golf; we don't work at golf. We're here to have some fun."

So what's it like to hit a golf ball 350 yards?

"You know," says Brian, "it's funny. When you really catch one, just absolutely clock it, it feels like you're just trying to smooth a little wedge out there, because everything is just so in synch and effortless. And for me, I get almost all my distance in the air, and I love to watch the ball stay up there in the air for seven or eight seconds."

"Yeah," he adds, "that's the fun part."

Gravel Acres Golf Club

JOHN FARMER, DALE LaVALLEY, JIM BREMAN
JACK HAHN, JIM BURRETT AND LEONARD ROSS
PACIFIC CREEK, WYOMING

"Two years in a row, the grizzly bears took an aversion to our greens and our flags, and they ripped out the flag and the cup with it – just tore it right out." *(Dale LaValley)*

"It isn't hard to do. The only thing is you have to live to be eighty to get a hole in one." *(Jim Breman)*

"The thing about golf is that every golfer - no matter how new at the game - is going to hit a shot that Tiger Woods would like to have. If you sink a twenty-foot putt, that's as good as he can do. You just don't do it as often as he does." *(Jim Burrett)*

They gloss over their real nature by describing themselves with such innocuous terms as "a family" or "a community" or "just neighbors and friends." But you begin to glimpse the dark truth when 57-year-old John Farmer reveals why he took up golf two summers ago: "The reason I got started was that these gentlemen around here won't talk to you unless you play golf."

Obsession? Addiction? Dysfunction? Just listen to 59-year-old Dale LaValley describe an intriguing pastime he calls "snow golf."

"That's the most fun," he says. "The crust gets very firm in the spring, firm enough to walk on. It's maybe three or four feet deep, and you can walk on it up until eleven o'clock or maybe twelve noon. What you do is pick a tree for a target - maybe 150 yards away, maybe 300 yards away - and as soon as you hit it in the tree well, then you're like in the hole."

Eighty-year-old Jim Breman adds that some years the crust is better than others but that you can't count on it being firm enough until April. "The real trick," he says, "is knowing when to get off. Because if you fall through, it's hard to get out again."

Jim Burrett remembers the exact day he first held a club. "It was April 15th of '94' because I just mailed in my income tax, and Rich and Jim came by and told me they wanted to play on the crust. So I humored them, and I've been playing ever since."

So where does this group of retirees play in the "off-season," when the ground's not covered in a frozen crust? "Well," explains Breman, "after we got hooked playing on the crust, we built a little course in the community - a nine-hole course. It's all gravel, except the greens; the greens are sand."

Low maintenance, anyway, you'd think. But 74-year-old Jack Hahn mentions one groundskeeping

difficulty: grizzly bear tracks. "We get lots of them – great big ol' tracks. And the thing is, everybody wants to see them, so we don't like to smooth them out."

Actually, most of the group's summertime rounds are now played on grass. "After we'd got to where we wouldn't embarrass ourselves," Breman explains, "we started playing the different courses around here."

That suited 90-year-old Leonard Ross, whose knees are no longer up the challenge of gravel and crust courses but who isn't about to abandon the game that took hold of him in his seventies. "I started playing when I turned seventy. Before that I thought golf was the dumbest thing I ever heard of – hit a ball and go look for it. Now I play at least once a week, sometimes twice. It's fascinating, and frustrating. I love the game."

Back to John Farmer, whose alternatives, you'll remember, were to take up the game or face social ostracism: "The nice thing about this group is that nobody takes it too seriously. Nobody's out here to kill anybody. We're just out here to have a good time, to enjoy the game, to be outdoors."

Right.

Gil Boggs

SPECIAL EVENTS MANAGER / FORMER PRINCIPAL DANCER WITH THE AMERICAN BALLET THEATER
THE GOLF CLUB AT CHELSEA PIERS
NEW YORK, NEW YORK

"It's funny. It's so easy for me to stand on one leg and turn around ten times, but to hit a golf ball straight is almost impossible."

Chelsea Piers is an interesting place: a four-level driving range built over a pier, with thirteen stations per level; outdoors, but heated, and operational year-round. Inside is an academy, staffed by PGA professionals, featuring three hitting stations equipped with video cameras for complete swing analysis.

But in terms of being out of the ordinary, the facility pales in comparison to its Special Events Manager, Gil Boggs. Growing up as a high school athlete in South Georgia in the 1970s, Gil went on to become a principal dancer in the American Ballet Theater. "In that time and place, boys really didn't take ballet," says Gil. But when he was ten years old he saw a friend perform in a local show, and he was fascinated. "By about fifteen," he says, "I know that this was how I wanted to make my living."

Having retired from the ballet company last July, he now has his sights firmly fixed on his next career. "I'm trying to pass the PAT (Players' Ability Test) so that I can become a PGA-sanctioned golf instructor." He's taken the test once and calls it "an enlightening experience." Depending on the difficulty of the course, you have to shoot a 76 or 77

twice in one day. His work in the theater taught him how to perform under pressure, Gil says, "but it's amazing in golf how your muscles can tense up. Now I'm playing on what I call the PAT Tour."

Already a seven-handicapper, Gil will reach his goal. In fact, he relishes the singular challenges and demands that golf imposes. He embraces the stern integrity of the game. "It's so easy," he says, "when you find your ball sitting in a divot, to say, 'Hey, I'm in the fairway, I don't have to hit out of a divot.' But you do have to hit the ball out of the divot! Golf teaches you that there's always a little obstacle there, but you can overcome it."

There are occasional rewards. On the par-three 17th at Pebble Beach, with a 35-mile-an-hour wind in his face, Gil pulled out his driver. "I was sure I had hit the green, but we couldn't find the ball. Then I figured I had gone over and into the water, or maybe into the rough, which was really high. No ball anywhere, so I go back and start looking in front of the green. One of my friends says, 'Did you look in the hole?' As I walk up I see a ball mark about three feet in front of the hole. I peer in and the word 'Hogan' is staring me in the face. I just collapsed on the green."

Barney Adams

CEO, ADAMS GOLF
ORLANDO, FLORIDA

"Sometimes you thin the ball and it rolls up five feet from the cup. You didn't deserve it. Sometimes you hit it perfect and the wind comes up and buries it in the trap. You didn't deserve that either. But that's life!"

Funny how some people just figure it out, just get the picture.

For Barney Adams, it was a simple truth: "I learned I had no future in selling a product. But if I could learn how to sell a service, the product would get sold in the process."

The product was golf clubs. Barney had bought the assets of Dave Pelz Golf in 1986 and began designing clubs. In 1991, he says, he moved his company to Dallas, into a facility exactly half as small as the trade show booth he's sitting in to tell this story. But in the meantime he had taught himself the art of custom fitting.

Click.

"Once I started custom fitting," says Barney, "the same clubs that nobody would look at the day before, now they're buying them. All the objections went away – they're too expensive, they're too whatever – because the service of custom fitting was so powerful."

Not that he was on easy street quite yet. Barney would travel around the country, set up shop on driving ranges and golf courses, and custom fit on Saturdays and Sundays. He'd sell his equipment on the spot and use the money to keep the company going.

Then came the next evolution in his "service drives product" philosophy.

"Everywhere we went, I got asked one question: 'Can you please help me with my long irons?' The oversized woods, with the ball sitting on the ground, do not look very hittable to most golfers, and they had problems with their long irons, so a lot of people were getting frustrated.'"

"The Tight Lies line," Barney continues, "was developed strictly to go along with my fitting system, to let me do a better job for my customers. Provide more service, if you will."

But then something new and unexpected happened. The phone began to ring. "And when the calls started coming in," says Barney, "we thought, 'Gee, maybe we got a product here that retails.'"

The rest, as they say, is history.

The former 1-handicapper admits that running his now huge business has cut into his playing time, but it seems a small price to pay: "Yeah, my game suffers, but I don't much care. Because I'm one of the very lucky people in the world who get to go to work and do what they really like to do. That's a neat place to be."

Karen Jacobs

DIRECTOR OF INSTRUCTION, JIM MCLEAN GOLF ACADEMY
SCOTTSDALE, ARIZONA

"It's the pursuit of perfection, and facing the fact that you are never going to attain it."

Karen Jacobs grew up playing all sports and was surrounded by brothers who did likewise. But when she first picked up a golf club at age sixteen, she fell in love and never looked back. Today she's a teaching pro in the golf mecca knows as Scottsdale.

Karen says what she loves best about her work is "the challenge of analyzing a golf swing." No two swings are alike, so every student renews the challenge. The reward for a teacher is in knowing that you can suggest a small adjustment "and make somebody better at the game, have them enjoy it more."

Karen describes golf as "an ongoing discipline," an ideal best exemplified by one of her current students: "He's close to eighty years old, still shoots in the 70s, practices every day, plays four or five times a week, still takes lessons, still working on his golf swing – a great, great, person who truly loves the game."

Working on their swing – certainly all of Karen's students have that much in common. Like Mary Deniger, for instance, whose job as a pension fund executive lends urgency to her desire to improve. "I have to play a lot of corporate golf," she says, "and I don't want to be too pathetic." Paying the ultimate tribute to her teacher, Mary recalls a recent game with friends at the Arizona Biltmore: "We were having trouble, so we pulled out our notes from Karen's lesson and were going over them right there on the tee box. It really helped."

Then there's Kathy Trn, who began playing a year ago and discovered Karen through a friend. To date, her best moment in golf was when her ball hit a palm tree and landed on the green. She, too, is working on her swing, getting better, and seeing herself improve, she says, "definitely keeps me coming back."

At a much different level is Tana Sackett, whose father is former tour player, Al Mengert. Tana has been playing since the age of five, and she knows well the hard-to-define but surpassing pleasure of hitting a golf ball flush: "Intuitively, you know you've hit it good, and it ends up going exactly where you wanted it to go when you hit it. You don't have a lot of control in this game, so to get that feeling is really neat."

Tana has caddied for her father at the British Seniors at Turnbury. She's met Arnold Palmer. She's friends with many of the women on the ladies' tour. But just like Kathy and Mary, she's still working on her swing. "The challenge of the game never diminishes. You're always trying to improve. I think that's how all golfers feel, even at the professional level. Always trying to improve."

David Wolper

Television Producer, Wolper Productions
Bel-Air Country Club
Los Angeles, California

"You know, any attractive woman who shoots in the 70s would rule the world."

David Wolper is the man who almost got away.

"When I was a youngster, playing in New York City," he recalls, "I would cost me about $200 to join a club and maybe $20 a month. I came to California and walked into one of the clubs and they said, 'That'll be $50,000 to join.' I said, 'Thanks anyway, I'm giving up golf. I quit golf from the age of 17 to the age of 60.'"

Ah, but at age 60.... "I absolutely went crazy," says David. "It was 1984, and I had done the opening and closing ceremonies for the Olympic Games. I was hot all over town, so I figure the time is right. I joined three golf clubs. I got on the USGA Foundation Board, on the Commissioner's Board of the LPGA. I produced an hour-long documentary on the hundred-year history of golf in America and a half-hour film on the thirteen greatest golfers of the 20th century."

From his work on those films, David has concluded that the great golfers have two things in common. First, they started young; and, second, they have "enormous concentration." Why can't Nicklaus putt or chip as well as he could 30 years ago? "It's all concentration," says David. "30 years ago all he had to think about was golf. Today he has to think about his business, his grandkid's got a cold, he forgot about some course he's supposed to do, maybe he's got to do an ad for a shirt tomorrow. Concentration is what you lose when you get older."

But for the last 15 years, David has done a pretty good job of concentrating on golf, and as a reward for his enthusiastic return to the game, golf has granted him some special moments. His favorite came at Augusta.

"We got to play right after the Masters," he recalls. "It was the year Fred Couples hit that ball on 16 into the side of the hill and it didn't roll back into the water. It stayed up on the bank, and he chipped it up and made his par. When I get to that hole, the same thing happens – my ball hits the hill, rolls down and stops about where Freddie's did. I walk up, chip onto the green and make the putt. So I look at my friends and say, 'What's so great about Fred Couples. I just made a three, too. Me and Freddie.'

"That Christmas, one of the guys got a picture of Freddie making his shot and had it framed with a little note saying, 'What's so hard about this?'"

Eddie Merrins

HEAD GOLF PROFESSIONAL
BEL-AIR COUNTRY CLUB
LOS ANGELES, CALIFORNIA

"Golf is the ultimate expression of our ineptitude, which we have to deal with."

Eddie Merrins has come a long way from Meridian, Mississippi. The road led first to LSU, where he held a golf scholarship; then to the Marion Golf Club in Philadelphia, his first position as a pro; then to the Rockaway Hunting Club on Long Island, with off-season teaching stints at Thunderbird in Palm Springs and at New York's Westchester Country Club.

"Being a golf professional," says Eddie, "is a lot like being an itinerant preacher. You never know where you might get called next." But Eddie's next call turned out to be his last one. In 1962 he accepted the position as head pro at the Bel-Air Country Club in Los Angeles, and he's been there ever since. "I came here to succeed Joe Novak, who had arrived in 1927. We're the only two professionals in the history of the club – 73 years."

During his tenure at Bel-Air, Eddie moonlighted for 14 years as the golf coach at UCLA, where his revival of the erstwhile dormant program culminated in the 1988 NCAA championship. His success as a coach grew naturally out of his love of teaching, but Eddie says that at first he was a bit puzzled by the concept of "coaching" golf. "It caught me off-guard," he says. "I'd never been addressed as 'Coach.' But ultimately the real meaning of the word occurred to me. It derives from putting the words 'coax' and 'teach' together. And that's how I approached it."

Whether coaxing or teaching, Eddie tries to get his students to take the "yes-I-can" approach. "The lesser player dwells on the negative – I'm going to hit it in the water; I'm going to three-putt – while the good player looks for the positive solution to the problem."

And the good player doesn't look back. "I've got as many bogeys – and worse – in my background as anybody," Eddie says. "But I'm hoping to make enough pars and birdies, and an occasional eagle, so that my final scorecard tallies out pretty well."

Eddie finds rich parallels between golf and the game of life. "Golf is an expression of the quest in all of us," he says. "We're all questing for something. We may never get there, but you can't take the quest away from us."

Looking at it another way, Eddie imagines everybody being issued a handicap. "Say your 'life' handicap is 14, who wouldn't want to become a 13, a 12, a 10, or ultimately a 'scratch' person? That's what it's all about, working to make yourself better."

Paul Andersen and Randy Udall

"Wild Golf"
Carbondale, Colorado

"There's a philosophy behind golf that's deeper than just the game itself. It's the idea of possibility in life. And you experience it with every swing." (Paul Andersen)

". . . people who don't play golf look at golfers as lunatics. They see the absurdity, but they don't see the beauty or the passion of the game." (Randy Udall)

Randy Udall and Paul Andersen have taken the game of golf to a whole new level – literally and metaphorically. In the first place, their "course" lies roughly 7,500 feet above sea level, at the base of Colorado's Mt. Sopris, so that, as Randy says, "it feels like you're playing on a kind of plateau, with the horizon visible 360 degrees." And in the second place, the course is no course at all but rather two square miles of shaggy pasture land.

What Randy and Paul call "Wild Golf" might more accurately be called "anti-golf": "You can tee off in any direction," says Randy. "There are no flags, no putting greens. There is no end point; the course can have nine holes, twelve holes, six holes. Except for the fact that there are no holes. We've taken away the holes."

And, of course, they've taken away the rules. They play by picking a tree in the distance, then driving, ironing, and chipping until they hit it. Then it's on to the next "hole."

If this sounds so little like golf as we know it as to be unrecognizable, Randy is quick to point out what every golfer will acknowledge as the essential similarity: "You're still looking for that sweet spot, still hunting that perfect swing."

For Paul, Wild Golf brought peace to an embattled psyche. "Frankly, to me, golf always seemed an environmental insult, a blight on the land, a private pastime for the rich, an elitist game, an abomination. Then our book club read Michael Murphy's Golf in the Kingdom, and in the interest of discussion of the book, I played a round at River Valley Ranch in Carbondale."

Big mistake. Paul quickly found himself "developing an affection for golf." On a bike ride through the mountains of Colorado he tried to explain his predicament to a friend. "I felt it was a real conflict deep inside me; part of me couldn't justify playing golf and another part just couldn't let it go. My friend motioned with his arm to a beautiful cattle pasture we were riding beside and said, 'Why don't you play

here?' I realized that was the answer: the grass was short-cropped; you could hit the ball a long way and still find it; you were out in nature, and there were no chemicals on the gound."

Randy's story had a different beginning. When he was in high school, thirty years ago, he was a six-handicapper. But a career as an outdoorsman – mountaineer, wilderness guide, environmentalist – left neither time nor inclination to hold onto this passion of his boyhood. For all those years the clubs stayed in the closet, until just last year Paul called to say, "Come out here. I want to show you something." And there it was, still: "I was immediately struck again by how sweet hitting a golf ball can be."

Needless to say, his return to the game didn't sit well with his circle of associates and coworkers: "Golf, in our part of the world, is the least politically correct sport right now, and these people I've hiked and run rivers with are just astounded that I'm playing golf again. It's as if I've taken up cocaine or heroin. I mean, they want to have an intervention or call in a therapist."

But it was too late. Randy had fallen off the wagon bigtime. "You know, golf is made wonderful by its inherent difficulty, and when you hit a golf ball well . . . there's no feeling that quite compares with it. It's incredibly fleeting, but very addictive."

And even more now than ever, thirty years later, in the middle of a pasture, where a round of golf might go like this: "We might play two or three holes, then pull out a small cook-stove and make a pot of tea. We'd drink a cup of tea and eat a cookie and smoke a cigarette, play a couple of more holes, then maybe take a swim in the river." This is a game without the "stifling conventions" of normal golf, a game where "the only strictures are the ones you want to create."

Ridiculous, say the purists. "That's the point," says Randy. "Wild Golf perfectly encapsulates the beautiful absurdity of the game."

Adds Paul: "It's so incongruous for me and Randy to play golf at all that the people we know are just amazed. Wild Golf makes it a little more feasible. It's the only rationale that flies."

Darius White and Steve Anti

BAG BOYS
TALKING STICK GOLF CLUB
SCOTTSDALE, ARIZONA

"The ball just sits there, and everybody knows the fundamentals of the swing. But actually doing it — hitting the perfect drive, chipping it close — it's all between the ears." (Steve Anti)

Couple of guys just trying to "work their way up" at Scottsdale's Talking Stick Golf Club. Darius, 21 years old, is an Outside Service Professional — starter, club-scrubber, bag guy, gofer. Steve, a little older, is a Player Service Professional, meaning that his job includes some clubhouse duty. Both are looking into the distant future, following cart paths that will slope steadily upward, they hope, until they find themselves as head pros or directors of golf.

Not PGA Tour stars, mind you. Not even in their dreams. Just day-laborers at the game of golf. Why? Well, why not? After all, golf is life.

"I was playing the fifth hole at Camelback," says Darius, "a 440-yard par four. Hit a terrible drive, still had 240 to the green. I took out my driver again, hit it off the fairway, and the ball rolled up onto the green and hit the stick. Didn't go in, but I had about a one-inch putt for birdie. There's nothing like hitting a bad shot and then hitting a great shot to recover. For me, that's what it's all about."

Steve tells a different story. He's been struggling to pass the Players' Ability Test, where — assuming standard course difficulty — you've got to shoot 76 or better twice in one day. It's a huge hurdle; once you pass, you're officially in the PGA program and can start giving lessons and moving up the ranks.

"I missed it by one stroke," Steve says. "I just needed to make par on 18 — this was my 36th hole — and I barely missed a six-footer on the low side. At the time I thought, 'This isn't the way it's supposed to happen.' But you know what, at least I was in the hunt."

Given where they are, and where they hope to be, it's no wonder that both credit golf with teaching them the virtue of patience.

"It teaches you how to grind," says Darius.

Steve puts it more philosophically: "Take what you're given. If you're playing a little cut shot off the tee, stick with it instead of trying to fight it. Play the game you've got that day."

But always, always, at the end of the grind, shimmering, evanescent . . . lies the grail.

"It's the pursuit of perfection," says Steve. "You'll never get there. You can get better and better, like Duval shooting 59, but perfection is unattainable. But still, we're driven to pursue it."

"Nobody's going to shoot an 18," adds Darius with a chuckle.

Alice Cooper

MUSICIAN
BILTMORE GOLF CLUB
SCOTTSDALE, ARIZONA

"I was from Detroit. There were three sports – baseball, football, and grand theft auto. All highly competitive, all involving running. We didn't think much about golf."

They say that golf teaches patience. The truth is, golf is patient. The game will wait as long as it has to.

In the case of Alice Cooper, it waited 30 years. "We were just sitting around drinking one day, when one of the guys said he was going to go play golf. I went along, just to get out of the house. I put my hands around a 7-iron and hit it 150 yards right down the middle. Had never touched a club in my life. Next day I bought a set and came back out, and I've probably played five days a week since then."

Today he's on the Callaway staff as a player advisor. In every city he tours, Callaway picks him up in the morning and takes him to the golf course; then he does his show that night. Still, Alice Cooper the musician and Alice Cooper the golfer present a bit of an incongruity: "Oh yeah, it's two worlds. I can play golf with the president of U.S. Steel, some guy with a gray suit and a Rolls Royce. But I guarantee, if I don't beat him it'll be an oddity."

Now a very low handicapper, Alice admits he's gotten some good help. Johnny Miller worked with him on his iron play, and he gives special credit to

John Daly. I spent a few days with Daly just chipping and putting. He taught me two or three shots I never knew existed, and my handicap dropped from 7 to about 3. He just shaved the strokes off around the green."

Having shot a 67 – his best round ever – one day and an 86 the next, Alice knows well the masochism buried in the heart of every golfer. "You're your own worst enemy out there," he says. "You can be playing great, and somebody'll say, 'Do you know where your hands are up there?' or maybe 'Do you exhale when you hit the ball?' and you're totally screwed."

Alice also speaks eloquently of the absolute integrity the game inspires. The way the pros play, routinely calling penalties on themselves for infractions which only they themselves witnessed, makes them seem like "Knights of the Round Table."

"You get in situations," he says, "where you think, 'I'll just bend the rules a little bit,' but then you think about the golf game. You can't bend the rules. You play it down. If you shoot 87 instead of 86, so what? You're still an honest man."

Bill Foster

VP, Bear Stearns
On the Subway
New York, New York

"The three things I missed the most during my two years in Hong Kong were my mom, American food, and golf – not necessarily in that order."

Bill Foster.
Case #246-113-748

History:

Hockey player in college. With teammates, played some golf in off-season. Mentioned similarity between slapshot and golf swing. Four years ago, received first set of clubs from fiancée as Christmas present. (Interesting aside: note role of fiancée as "enabler.") Played twelve times that year. Increasing frequency. Defining moment: once chipped in from off the green on three holes in a row. Now carries clubs on subway to local courses and driving ranges.

Symptoms:

Describes golfing urge using terms such as "addiction" and "obsession." Claims to be cultivating the standard golfing virtues of patience and humility. Speaks frequently of compulsion created by having hit "that one good shot." Now participates in annual golfing weekend with buddies, calling the event "a weekend I will look forward to every year for the rest of my life."

Diagnosis:

Common Golf Syndrome.

Prognosis:

Poor.

David Liniger, Owner, and Jim Engh, Designer

THE SANCTUARY
CASTLE ROCK, COLORADO

Dave Liniger and Jim Engh traveled widely divergent routes to wind up inhabiting the same paradise.

Dave, the founder of RE/MAX, never once played the game until after he had bought the property on which he would build The Sanctuary. After years of watching the golfers at Castle Pines, where he lived on the tenth fairway, he finally succumbed and joined the club. As soon as he took up the game, the realization struck him: his "unique piece of land," bordered on all four sides by forty thousand acres of open space but still just fifteen minutes from Denver's southern suburbs, "would make a fantastic golf course."

Jim, meanwhile, the son of an amateur champion, was born with golf in his blood. Not even a near-fatal golf cart accident when he was two (he managed to step on the accelerator and flip the cart while his dad was making a shot) could cool his ardor for the game, and designing courses became his livelihood.

When Dave realized what his property was meant to be, he had the good fortune to find a designer whose sensibility matched his own. Both men emphasize that golf should be a supremely visual experience.

"I love the outdoors," says Dave. "I love wildlife, nature's solitude, spectacular views. And one of the things Jim and I talked about from day one was how we could make the course a succession of visual surprises. You can walk from the green to the next tee box and maybe see an elk or a golden eagle; you walk around the next bend and there's a beautiful waterfall. You weren't expecting it, but it's totally natural. It fits right in."

For his part, Jim talks about "creating a space," an experience for the senses that's much greater than just a matter of how you score. "The golf course should be a journey," he says, "actually eighteen individual journeys. This is what sets golf apart from other sports and makes it so popular." The visual component, for Jim, is "very powerful" - especially at a place like The Sanctuary.

"The biggest challenge here," he says, "was to maintain the natural setting because the beauty of this site was phenomenal. The more rugged the site, the harder it is to construct and design, but the more spectacular it is in completion. And this was by far the most difficult project I've ever undertaken."

No wonder they couldn't decide what to do with it when they were finished. "We knew we didn't want houses," says Dave, "since that would have spoiled the natural beauty, and we didn't think we wanted the typical membership." Their decision was to keep it completely private, but to make it a valuable community resource by opening it up for charity tournaments. "That way," he says, "people get to play it like it was meant to be, when there might only be six or seven foursomes on the course the entire day, and each individual player feels like he has the whole place to himself."

Bill Kubly

President, Landscapes Unlimited
Fleming Island Golf Course
Orange Park, Florida

"What I really love is the people of the game of golf. Not just the players but the distributors of irrigation equipment, the distributors of heavy equipment, the owners, the managers – all the people who like this sport. It's just a neat group of people."

Bill Kubly went to work for a golf course construction firm as soon as he graduated from the University of Wisconsin with a degree in landscape architecture. Thirty years later, he's still in the business. "I always had a love of golf," he says, "but I didn't realize how much of a love I had."

In 1976, he started his own company, Landscapes Unlimited, "with a pickup truck, a pipe wrench, and a rented trencher." It was definitely a one-man shop. "Today," says Bill, "we have in excess of one thousand employees working on up to forty projects at any one time throughout the country."

How does one man keep track of forty projects going on at the same time? The secret is a physics concept called jet propulsion. "The Lear jet allows us to get to two or three places a day, then get back home. We call it our time machine. Without it, it would be real hard to have any kind of family life."

Bill admits to being lucky to have come along when he did. "When I first got involved," he says, "I figured I had over-specialized. Back in 1971 I thought maybe the business would last about ten or twelve years. It turns out, of course, that golf development has gone totally berserk."

There are two kinds of golf course architects, according to Bill. There are those who plan meticulously, and then there are those whom Bill calls "the arm-wavers." Both kinds can create wonderful golf courses, but Bill has sometimes gotten frustrated working with the second type. "I built one TPC course, for example, where we put a fairway bunker in five or six locations, then ended up with it back where it started."

But working alongside the game's great architects has been one of Bill's keenest pleasures. "Tom Fazio, Robert Trent Jones, Reese Jones, Tom Weiskopf – it's just a real thrill to work with people like that and have them respect what we do."

Bill's business philosophy is a reflection of what he considers the spirit of the game. "What makes golf stand out is the honesty and integrity of the game, and that has spilled over into our business. The golf course construction/design business is such a close-knit group that you have to have total integrity at all times. If you don't, it will catch up with you in a hurry."

The result is that Bill gets to work with other people who feel the same way he does — "the kind of people you want to be around every day." And for that, he says, "I thank my lucky stars."

Tom Simonson

STARTER
SAND HILLS GOLF CLUB
MULLEN, NEBRASKA

"I bet the old boy who owned it probably turned over in his grave when he saw that golf course coming. I've got to admit, though, it's a heck of a golf course."

Also, grill-master at the clubhouse snack bar, where word has it that he makes the world's greatest hamburgers. And who knows? Maybe he makes them out of his own beef, since 71-year-old Tom Simonson is actually a lifelong rancher who still runs a small herd every year.

In fact, Tom still works the same land his father settled in 1905 and lives in the same house he was born in.

It's a good life in the American heartland.

Tom sold off part of his ranch in the late '80s and was on hand a few years later when Sand Hills began to be developed. "It was just ranch land then," he says, and we went out there to tear out the fences."

He started working regularly in 1994 and, in his words, did a little bit of everything: "First of all I started fencing in the golf course itself. And then we worked at putting in the electricity, water lines - just about whatever it takes to build a golf course."

With all the back work completed, Tom assumed his current positions as starter and grill chef. For the latter post he makes no claims as to his qualifications: "I just kind of fell into cooking the hamburgers accidently because somebody needed to do it and I

happened to be the one there." And even though he admits the burgers are particularly good, he'll take no credit for himself: "We get good beef up here."

Tom was no stranger to golf, though, even before his Sand Hills days. He started playing back in the '60s on a local course that, back then, had sand greens. After the ranch work was done, he would meet his buddies for nine holes or so almost every day of the week.

These days he plays very little. "I just don't have time," he says, "or else I'm just too tired or lazy at the end of the day. Now it's just an occasional Sunday afternoon when the Sand Hills course isn't too busy. Tom has vivid memories of long-ago days when the golf course was still ranch land. "I used to ride my horse out there when I was a kid, and in high school I worked for the guy that owned it – weeding the cattle, taking cattle to market. We'd sometimes have to skip school on a Friday and take a couple days to get to the railroad. We'd take our time because we didn't want to take any fat off of them."

"Yeah," he continues, "I bet the old boy who owned it probably turned overin his grave when he saw that golf course coming. I've got to admit, though, it's a heck of a golf course."

Jim Chaffin

MANAGING PARTNER
OLD TABBY LINKS AT SPRING ISLAND, NORTH CAROLINA

"It is very important that there be a rhythm, if you will, to the golf experience. Part of that is the flow of the holes and the type of shots that they require. But the other part of it is the rhythm of the nature around you. Is it a soothing, natural place?"

"I'm really old-fashioned about the game of golf," says Jim Chaffin, expressing a sentiment shared by perhaps too few golf course developers. His attitude toward the game was shaped early on, in the little agricultural community in Virginia where he grew up. He earned money on weekends by caddying at the town's nine-hole golf course, "laid out on the rolling hills that nature had presented there," where, after each hole, he would drag the sand green with a piece of carpet to prepare it for the next foursome.

Looking back on that experience – the "great caddy master," the demeanor of the players, the natural beauty of the landscape – Jim says today, "Golf was a gift to me. . . . I have deep gratitude for all the people who protected the essence of the game, who kept it unpretentious and low-key and dedicated to civil behavior ."Fundamental to golf's enduring appeal, according to Jim, is the simple fact that it is played outside. "From the standpoint of course design," he says, "we want people – no matter their skill level – to be challenged by the experience and enriched by the environment in which the game is played."

No wonder, that, Spring Island, combines all he has learned about both community planning and conservation. "Spring Island is really a park with a community in it as opposed to a community with a park in it. Our dream was to have a community where all of the man-made facilities were subservient to the natural beauty already here." Jim finds it gratifying that the members often use the Spring Island course as a nature walk.

A natural philosopher in the old sense of the phrase, Jim sees the relevance to golf of E. O. Wilson's "Biophilia Hypothesis" – the concept that good health depends upon a connection to the out of doors – and uses Thoreau to help explain the profound allure of the game: "Golf calls us to go confidently in the direction of our dreams – our dreams of that perfect round – even though we realize that perfection is unattainable.

But in assessing what golf means to his life, Jim returns to the idea of the gift – though the reward he has in mind may not be the one we're looking for when we're pressing on the back nine on Sunday afternoon: "The thing to remember is that the reward for all your persistence, for all your practice, for all your playing, is not really a great score or a great shot, but what you become by it."

Charlie Jones

VETERAN NBC SPORTS ANNOUNCER
LA JOLLA, CALIFORNIA

"The thing about golf is, with other sports you can count on your opponent to make some mistakes. The golf course never makes any mistakes."

As soon as his voice changed, Charlie Jones applied for work as a radio announcer. The station manager got him to read for a few minutes and hired him on the spot. "I asked him when he wanted me to start," recalls Charlie, "and the man said, 'Right now!' So I told him in words worthy of some Hall of Fame biography, 'I can't. My mother is waiting out in the car.'"

But after taking him home and feeding him a peanut butter sandwich, his mom returned him to the station, and at one o'clock that same day his career was launched. "I'm very lucky," says Charlie. "I got to do exactly what I wanted to do. It was a lot of fun."

Charlie's first golf work came in 1964 – the America Classic in Akron, Ohio. "These days," he says, "the announcers sit inside the glass booth and all that. But back then, we were really outside; there was just a scaffolding. So we really did have to whisper."

They also got close to the athletes, and Charlie became good friends with Arnold Palmer. "I was his guest in Latrobe once, after the World Series of Golf, and of course we were going to play golf the next morning. I can't sleep. I'm a nervous wreck. I mean, I'm a sixteen or eighteen. So we go out the next morning, and I'm all over the course. Just awful. At about the fourth tee Arnold puts his arm around my shoulder and says, 'Charlie, I don't care how you play. I only care how I play. Just have a good time.' I'll never forget that. Because it's so true about golf."

What, exactly, is so true about golf, explains Charlie, is that "it's you against yourself – just you and the course." He remembers an afternoon from the past summer when he was by himself, hitting it really well on the range, and decided to play nine. "It's Thursday, no one around. Again, I'm an eighteen. After six holes, I'm one under par. Everything has come together – I'm swinging well, putting well, seeing well, good rhythm, everything. Only two people know I'm one under. That's God and me. And we both know I've got three holes to go. I finish double bogey, double bogey, double bogey. Holy cow! How can you choke when there's nobody there but you and the golf cart?"

"But that's golf," says Charlie. 'I'll never do this again,' you say. And your next sentence is, 'What time tomorrow?'"

Johnny Henry

GOLF MEMORABILA COLLECTOR
ENNIS, TEXAS

"When I was young, I played with the caddies. We didn't have any money. In fact, I had to go find a ball before I could play. We'd play for thumps on the head. You gotta play for something."

For most of his 72 years Johnny Henry has lived and breathed golf. Now, sitting in his large, high-ceilinged den, "just crammed full" of golf clubs dating back to the early 1800s, he's literally surrounded by the game.

He's been involved at every level: outstanding amateur player, course architect, irrigation system designer, greenskeeper (this later in life, at Brook Hollow in Dallas, which Johnny describes as "a fine old-money club with very little play and an unlimited budget"), and now Regional Director of the Golf Collector's Society.

He's loved every minute of it. As he says, "What better way to spend a day than to be in the outdoors with the birds singing and in the company of nice people." Then for emphasis: "Therein lies the secret of golf: you meet so many nice people involved in it."

For Johnny, the essence of the game is embodied in his story of David Ramsay, the elderly caddy at Carnoustie who "went around" with Johnny when he played there and with whom Johnny subsequently corresponded. When he made plans to return to Scotland, Johnny received a note from Mrs. Ramsay saying that Mr. Ramsay would love to see Johnny but that he had suffered a stroke and wouldn't be able to go around with him. He walks with a stick, she explained.

Johnny immediately sent Mr. Ramsay an aluminum-shafted driver on which he had inscribed Ramsay's name across the bottom of the sole plate and bent the handle for use as a walking cane. During their visit, Mr. Ramsay, in turn, presented Johnny with a beautiful wooden-headed, spliced-neck club made by the renowned Bobby Hewitt. Flabbergasted, Johnny tried to purchase the club, but Mr. Ramsay would have none of it: "I just want you to have it so that when you see it on your wall back in Texas, you'll be reminded of your dear friend in Scotland who loves you very much."

"That's what makes golf the game that it is," says Johnny.

Johnny enjoys helping others become knowledgeable collectors. It's his way of "paying back," of acknowledging his debt to the game that has given him so much.

"You know," he says, trying to sum it up, "women can be pretty emotional, but I really don't think they can understand the love you can have for the game of golf."

Win Padgett and John Crow Miller

MEMBERS, GOLF COLLECTORS SOCIETY OF AMERICA
BROOK HOLLOW GOLF CLUB
DALLAS, TEXAS

"Every time I take a swing, some old Scot is smiling down from heaven and saying, 'My club is in play. Keep your eye on the ball.'" (John Miller)

"I actually broke down on the fifth tee at Oakhurst; it's so overwhelming to realize you're in an environment that's exactly the same as it was 120 years ago." (Win Padgett)

Some people collect antique golf clubs and balls; Win Padgett and John Crow Miller play with them. In this singular endeavor they have found a way to pay homage to history of the game and at the same time to subdue their obsession with the score.

"Forgetting titanium and high-tech in favor of moving back toward the fount of the game offers its own spiritual reward every time I take a swing," John explains.

It can be a lonely pursuit, he concedes; most golfers have no idea what he's up to. Even caddies, says John, don't know which of these odd clubs – jiggers, mashees, niblicks – to pull out of the bag. Those who do know are likely to be members of the Golf Collectors Society, perhaps even among the devotees who make the annual pilgrimage to Oakhurst Links in West Virginia, the oldest links in America. Here, at their ancient shrine, says John, "we chase a gutta-percha ball over fairways tended by sheep on hilly ground that has been hosting golf since 1884." Members of the society, on both sides of the pond, "regard what the Scots did two centuries ago as the supreme art of the game. It should not be ignored."

"Oakhurst has all the elements of the old-time golf experience," adds Win. "The square sand tee boxes, the pails of water and sand that you mix together to form your tee on the teeing ground, fairways that we would consider essentially rough on a modern course, small greens, flagsticks three feet high."

For those who love the history of the game, this stepping back in time provides an unforgettable experience. "This is golf in its purest form," says Win. "You're walking, of course. Golf has always been a walking sport. You're carrying your clubs. They didn't even have bags back then. You carried, four, five, or six clubs under your arm or in your hand. You invent shots; you let go of your traditional concept of what an iron or graphite club might do under certain circumstances."

And you really learn what all golfers say golf teaches them: patience. "You can't force anything in golf anyway," says Win, "and you certainly can't in hickory golf. It's really a nice revisitation of the basic principles of the game, which are to play the course as you find it and the ball as it lies. That's the bedrock of hickory golf."

Admittedly, back home in Texas, John's friends are shocked at his current handicap (which used to be in the low single digits). "'Miller,' they ask, 'Why are you making a hard game harder?' I tell them I'm making a fun game funner."

Here is the deal, says John: "When I approach a par-5, I cannot reach it in regulation. That's a given, so it's no longer in my mind. As I approach my fourth shot, which hopefully is somewhere close to the green, I have hit three very thoughtful shots to get there. Nobody knows that but me, nor do they understand how I can walk off the green with a bogey and a smile on my face. But that's what hickory does. I no longer have to worry about being the best golfer in America. The pressure is off."

So . . . golf without the gnashing of teeth, without the hurling of clubs, without the ear-burning imprecations? John swears to have found it. "I have happily departed," he says, "from the pursuit of par."

George Peper

EDITOR-IN-CHIEF, Golf Magazine
NEW YORK, NEW YORK

"The wonder of the game is that you don't know what's over the next rise, around the next corner. For me, it's an adventure on every swing."

After graduating from Princeton with a degree in comparative literature, George Peper decided to head up to New Haven. "Two reasons," he says. "I thought I wanted to become Dr. Peper, Ph.D., and Yale has the best university golf course in the East."

The second turned out to be the more compelling. "By November the course was under snow, and I could see no legitimate reason to remain in New Haven. I went to my advisor to tell him I was thinking I should quit, and he immediately said, 'I think you're right.'"

So, says George, "I'm 22-years-old and have failed at the only thing I'd ever tried. I sat down and asked myself, what would I do if I could do anything in the world? It didn't take long to come to me. I'd be editor-in-chief of either *Golf Magazine* or *Golf Digest*. Swear to God. This was 1972."

The circuitous path he took toward his destination has made him a believer in serendipity. "I've found that if you're lucky enough to figure out exactly what it is you want, you don't have to be brilliant or even hard-driving, but you just have to keep pointing in that direction and eventually your path will connect with the right opportunity."

George has seen significant change at *Golf Magazine* in the 23 years he's been there, most of them guided by his own steadfast principle: "I don't work for *Golf Magazine* or for *Times-Mirror* Magazines or for some CEO in the corner office. I work for the readers. I'm their slave, their prostitute. I'm there to give them what they want."

The most radical re-engineering of the magazine's content came after George took a look at the huge group of baby boomers who would be taking up golf during midlife. What would they want? "We're selfish, we don't have a lot of time, and we're not big readers," he concluded. The result, in the magazine, was the concept of "the short 18 holes" – a 35-page section that used to have five long articles in it but that now has 18 two-page articles. "It was an immediate success," says George, "and spurred huge growth."

A lifelong player and low handicapper, George is quick to testify to golf's addictive power. "It's very much like gambling. Hitting a jackpot on a one-armed bandit is like hitting that one good shot. You're not going to walk away. You're convinced it'll happen again.

"Actually," he decides, "it's even better than gambling, because we're all convinced that we have some influence over the outcome."

Terri Hession and Cheri Carse

FOUNDER /CHAIRWOMAN AND MEMBER
GOLF WEASELS INTERNATIONAL
METRO WEST GOLF CLUB, ORLANDO, FLORIDA

"What's the hook that makes us shame and humiliate ourselves? The game is always there calling to you – the ultimate challenge and the most elusive victory. That's what keeps us coming back." (Terri Hession)

It's a simple concept. "A Golf Weasel is someone who is willing to make the ultimate sacrifice – family, friends, job, money, spouse, career advancement, any or all of those things – to play golf."

So says founder and chairwoman Terri Hession, who then explains how it works: "A person sacrifices one or all of these things to play a round of golf, then tells his or her story of the great sacrifice. If the story qualifies, we have a Weasel Induction Ceremony and the new member is welcomed into the club."

Member Cheri Carse offers her Weasel story as an example: "I worked for an engineering company, and the president was coming in and wanted to see me. But I had a Weasel qualifying date out here and I wasn't about to miss it. I called in sick, and then, because the president is also a member out here, actually used a different name that day so he couldn't find out I was out here when I was supposed to be sick."

As Terri points out, Weasels abide by a few binding rules: "A Weasel doesn't cheat the game. A Weasel can never say "no" to another Weasel to play a round of golf, short of illness. You cannot play another Golf Weasel for money. You must play for pride, humiliation, degradation."

However, there's also the matter of Weasel etiquette. "Weasels have their own Weasel Salute – you have to cry out 'EEE! EEE!' when you see another Weasel – and also the Weasel Handshake, which is the two Weasel claws hooking together. These are important," says Terri, "because even if it causes you shame and embarrassment, you must give the Weasel Salute."

Weasels now number 94, according to Terri, with 20 percent of the membership in the United Kingdom. "We run the gamut, including four knights among our U.K. members. And even though I'm the founder, only 10 percent of the members are women." In perspective, it's easy to see that Golf Weasels International is simply another expression – albeit a bizarre one – of the passion that golf elicits. Terri confirms this observation with the story of Bill Renns, one of her favorite Weasels: Bill was in critical condition after his fourth heart attack when Terri went to the hospital to visit him. "I was holding his hand, waiting for him to open his eyes. Finally he did and turned to me and said, 'Doc says six weeks before I can hit the putting green and maybe eight before I can go to the range.' The status report right away, you see. That passion is what kept him alive another 15 years."

Tico Torres

PERCUSSIONIST, BON JOVI
NEW YORK, NEW YORK

"Ernie Els told me, 'You know, for a drummer your timing's awful bad.'"

Bon Jovi percussionist Tico Torres has been a musician for thirty-three years and an artist since childhood.

He's been a golfer since that day twelve years ago when Willie Nelson invited him to the course he owned in Texas. "We're standing on the first tee, and there's a house down there along the fairway, and I say, 'Willie, what am I supposed to do?' He says, 'Well, if you hit the house, don't worry, because they shouldn't have built the goddamn thing on my golf course.'"

He was immediately hooked, not only by the game but by the mirror it holds up to the people playing it: "I was totally enthralled. I found out that you can immediately discover the character of the person you're playing with. You find out their integrity. You find out if they cheat, of if they cheat themselves, or if they're angry, or if they're happy – immediately! It's like a lie detector. And through that I can gauge my own self-being."

As for the game itself, Tico has an artist's appreciation of the mystery that lies at the heart of the well-executed golf shot. "Artists know that they must go back to the purity and simplicity of the child, who acts without preconceived thought. I think that's what you have to do to play golf – clear your mind and let it flow. I think your mind is your own worst enemy."

The result, says Tico, when "it all comes together without thinking about it, is that one shot that's complete poetry. It's that one shot that brings me back."

Tico has found another way – and a unique one – to bring his artist's sensibility to the game of golf. In his effort to learn more about the grip, Tico found a vacuum; there was absolutely no three-dimensional representation of how the best golfers held their clubs. So several years ago he began a project he calls The Majors Collection – bronze castings of the actual grips of the best players in the game. To date he's completed ten, including Nicklaus, Palmer, Player, Price, Els, and Ballesteros – each of which will be offered to sale in a very limited edition, with all proceeds going to the charity of the player's choice.

"My intent was to be able to look and the grip in its entirety," Tico says. "Three hundred sixty degrees. This was something you just couldn't get out of a book. Now maybe kids will be able to go to a museum and look at them."

For Tico, who not only is taking no compensation for the project but is in fact absorbing his own expenses, it's a way to give something back to the game. Plus, out of the experience he got a free golf lesson: "What it has taught me is that, basically, there's only one right grip – and they all have it."

Scott Sackett

EXECUTIVE DIRECTOR, RESORT GOLF GROUP
LEGEND TRAIL
SCOTTSDALE, ARIZONA

"We like to use the analogy of the duck swimming on the pond. The duck always looks calm on top of the water, but he's paddling like the devil underneath."

If you've been racing motocross professionally from the age of 19 to 24, travelling forty weeks out of the year and racing five or six days a week, then suddenly decide to quit and go back to school, well, you find that you've got time on your hands.

Scott Sackett decided to fill that time by playing golf. "I was used to a hectic schedule," he says, "and all of a sudden all I'm doing is taking four classes. I needed something to do." A friend invited him to play a round of golf, something he had done maybe fifteen times in his life.

He enjoyed it enough to seek out a part-time job picking up range balls at the local municipal course. Within a year, he was teaching the game.

How do you go from being a beginner to a teacher in a year? "Well," says Scott, "that first year I had my six-hour work shift, and then I'd play. I probably played 300 times that year. I also got a lot of good instruction."

Scott stayed at that municipal course for seven years, taught next at a driving range for three years, and then became Director of Schools for Jim McLean at Doral. Now, working out of Legend Trail in Scottsdale, Scott is Executive Director of the Resort Golf Group, a consortium of eighteen teaching facilities. He has also been selected as one of Golf Magazine's Top 100 Teachers for 1999-2000.

Unlike many teaching pros, Scott never gave much thought to making a living as a player. "A lot of people out here in the Southwest," he says, "are trying to teach and trying to play. But my feeling is that if you're trying to do both, you'll be mediocre at both. Now I play maybe twenty times a year."

Not that he doesn't miss it. "I played nine holes yesterday morning over at Eagle Mountain. I hadn't played for about two months. I got out there and thought, 'Why am I not doing this once a week?'"

As a teacher, Scott keeps his focus on the fundamentals. "With all the computers and stuff, instruction is getting complex. But we try to teach Golf 101, mastering the basics. And that is simply, grip, posture, alignment, and balance. If you have those four components in your swing and in your game, you will become a good player."

He also stresses that, in golf, good things happen and bad things happen, and that good players have learned to shrug off the bad shots and move on. "After all," he says, "the best players in the world hit only 71 percent of their shots where they mean to."

Jay Larson

SPEED GOLF CHAMPION
LOMAS SANTA FE EXECUTIVE COURSE
SOLANA BEACH, CALIFORNIA

"My goal in life has always been to do what I love; otherwise, I don't see the purpose."

The concept is simple enough. You take your score and your time on the course and add them together. "So if you shot an 80 in 60 minutes and 22 seconds," says Speed Golf world record holder Jay Larson, "your score would be 140.22.

Jay's current mark? "My record in the sport is even par 72 in 39 minutes and 55 seconds. So that's 111.55."

Excuse me?

It helps to know that Jay is both a former golf professional and a former professional triathlete, so Speed Golf would seem to be natural fit for his abilities. He also swears it's great fun.

Jay first played Speed Golf when he was among ten people – including world-class runners and PGA professionals who were into fitness – invited to a special event filmed by ESPN. He won that event and has been playing and promoting the sport ever since.

For Jay, Speed Golf puts all that he likes about sports into one package: "It appeals to the part of me that likes high-intensity sports as well as the calm aspect of a good round of golf." It's also a total test. "Hand-eye coordination, cardiovascular fitness,

muscular fitness – it's all required in Speed Golf. You have to be pretty complete in your athleticism to play the game."

Also, says Jay, Speed Golf forces you to do what you should be doing in regular golf anyway: trust yourself. "This is what all the sports psychologists are teaching the touring pros now: trust your first instinct, don't over analyze, just be an athlete." In Speed Golf, you don't have any choice. "Speed Golf is free from analysis. You have to just trust. This is the club that's going to work. Hit it! No time to think because the clock's running."

Jay isn't sure where Speed Golf will take him. Nor is he concerned about that. It's just what he enjoys doing right now, and the thousands of e-mails and phone calls he gets from fellow enthusiasts are simply an added bonus. "I saw 80 people come of the 18th green at Rancho Bernado in our first Speed Golf tournament, and I didn't see one scowling face or one thrown club or one unhappy person, no matter what they shot. They had both the endorphin high and the golf high all at once."

Considering the possibilities, Jay thinks, "I just may be ahead of my time."

Tom Fazio

GOLF COURSE DESIGNER
BEAVER CREEK, COLORADO

"People talk about signature holes. That's not my thing. My belief is that every hole needs to be a signature hole. Every golf course is a signature golf course."

Tom Fazio, arguably the world's foremost golf course architect, prefers to be called a golf course designer. "You think of architecture as such an exact science," he says, "whereas designer gives you a little bit more freedom and flexibility."

Tom clearly is more artist that scientist ("the Italian half of my heritage," he says), and it's no wonder that the concept of the "frame" is crucial to his vision of any golf hole. "We create golf holes in settings," he says, "standing on the tee, then on the landing area looking toward the green, and we want the picture in front of us to be balanced, to be beautifully framed."

If what you're looking for – the drama, the excitement, the feel – is not there in the setting, Tom says, then create it! "It used to be that a great piece of land was maybe the premier factor for having a great golf course. Today, in my opinion, it doesn't matter. Doesn't matter how good the land is, or how bad the land is. The only thing that counts is the end result." Tom loves to tell about building Shadow Creek in Las Vegas with Steve Winn. When he tried to explain to Steve that in Las Vegas there simply was no environment on which to build a great golf course, "Steve just looked at me and said, 'Well, why don't we create an environ-ment and put a golf course on it.' I thought, 'I have to work with this guy.'"

Tom grew up in a golfing family. His uncle, George Fazio, was a pro of considerable renown (he lost the 1950 U.S. Open in a playoff with Hogan and Al Mengert), and his father was an avid player who had Tom caddying for him before he was big enough to carry the bag. "I didn't mind that, though," says Tom. "The only thing I didn't like was I wouldn't get paid if Dad lost."

His uncle encouraged him to get into the course design business, and Tom has never looked back. "Never did anything else in my life. Never wanted to, and still don't want to do anything else." Being a great designer, he says, "takes passion, a love for the game, and most important, having it be the thing that you really want to do."

Tom recalls walking a piece of property in northern Michigan on an early November day. "It was a beautiful sunny day, and then suddenly clouds moved in and it started snowing. There I am, walking those hills and fields, imagining a golf course – the bright sun, then the snow – and I'm thinking, 'This is one of the greatest days of my life.'"

Tom Fazio is a man who found his calling.

The Chilly Open

WAYZATA, MINNESOTA

Peter Lambert is president of the Wayzata, Minnesota, Chamber of Commerce. He also happens to be presiding over the 16th Annual Chilly Open.

To paraphrase William Faulkner, the event has not merely endured; it has prevailed. "It's just blossomed over the years," says Peter, who is in his sixth year as a tournament official. "We now have 27 holes – three different nine-hole shotguns – and a total of 1,200 people out here on this frozen lake."

Doing what, exactly? "Well," says Peter, "you can take as many clubs as you want out onto the course. You hit a tennis ball and try to get it into the holes that have been drilled into the ice. Some holes have doglegs, some are straight-away, some longer than others."

Each hole, according to Peter, is created and sponsored by a different business in the community, and the entire event is designed to benefit a designated charity. Minnesota Food Shelves is this year's beneficiary.

But it's also a good excuse for the whole town to turn out and have fun. The sponsoring companies give their employees the day off, and everybody comes to either play or watch. "We even have a theme," says Peter. "This year it's 'Back to the Fifties,' so you'll see that manifested in the way people dress and design their holes. At our particular hole, we're handing out 'Leave It to Beaver' t-shirts."

Besides, what else are they going to do in the middle of a Minnesota February?

"Hey," says Chris Dolezal, one of the players, "We live in Minnesota. You've got to get outside once in a while. Golfing on ice is a nice change."

Especially when the weather "breaks," adds player Paula Schwichtenberg. "When it's nice like this, 20 to 30 degrees outside, it draws thousands of people. It's just a good time."

Any similarity to actual golf? "You immediately throw all your golf skills out the window," says Paula's husband, Dave. "If you take it seriously, your ball's going to go about five yards."

Peter agrees: "Here you have no expectations to worry about. As a result, the frustration level goes way down. Really, with all these obstacles people set up around their holes, this is more like miniature golf than real golf."

Mostly, everyone agrees, it's just a lot of fun.

Chris's wife Lauri sums it up: "The Chilly Open falls right between holidays. It's the perfect break in the middle of the winter."

Reg Murphy

PAST PRESIDENT, USGA
OCEAN FOREST GOLF CLUB
SEA ISLAND, GEORGIA

"Nothing ever quite matches the thrill of that first well-struck golf shot. Even if you're playing by yourself, and nobody else knows it. You don't need anybody else to know it."

In a relatively few years as an executive with the USGA, Reg Murphy left a lasting mark.

Reg was still the publisher of the Baltimore Sun in 1988 when the USGA decided to hold the Women's Open at Five Farms, at the Baltimore Country Club. By default, he says, he became the general chairman of the Open, and when it was successful he was asked to join the USGA's Executive Committee. Within a few years (1994) he had become the president.

"I should tell you," Reg says, "that before that time I had had no experience – none – with the USGA, except to read the rule book. And I barely knew how to read the rule book, to be honest with you."

Reg says he joined the association at a critical juncture, "at a time when it needed to think about what the future looked like." For one thing, at that time the USGA still insisted upon calling the people who joined "associates." As Reg remembers, "It took me three years to get the USGA to start calling its people 'members.' And over the next few years it went from having 150,000 associates to having 750,000 members. Now it's approaching one million."

Reg also saw the association's broadcast contract grow tremendously. With the increased revenue, the USGA now can make "significant numbers of grants around the country to programs like First Tee, to minority and inner city programs – these very important things that the association is now doing very well."

After all, Reg emphasizes, this is where golf's future lies. "Golf must grow at the level at which the Scots always thought it should grow, the common man's level. It has to grow at the unsophisticated level, not at the country club level. It's important that golf become a people sport again, just as it was in its origins."

If it were up to Reg, golf would loosen up, shed its elitist image. "If I were given the power and skill to be an architect, I would be out there building six-hole golf courses and twelve-hole courses – whatever fit the land. I'd be trying to entice people to come out and play a few holes, without worrying about either how beautifully the course was manicured or how nicely the players were dressed."

Reg readily admits to having played – and having enjoyed playing – the best courses all over the world. But that experience has only validated his notion of what golf is at heart: "It's a game to be enjoyed by common folk walking on common ground in all kinds of weather with all kinds of distractions. It doesn't need to be the rigid thing that some people, including me at times, have made it."

Laurie Frutchey

COURSE SUPERINTENDENT
BLACK DIAMOND RANCH
LECANTO, FLORIDA

"I love seeing a job through from start to finish. Even simple things like walk-mowing a green or hand-raking a trap – you know what it looks like when you start and what it looks like when it's finished. I find that rewarding."

It started as a part-time job, a way for a Florida State coed to earn a little extra money. "Mowing greens in the morning and raking traps – anything they'd let me do," says Laurie Frutchey.

She was studying biology, planning to be a high school science teacher. But the part-time job turned into a calling. Now Laurie is one of a small handful of female golf course superintendents in the country, and the two courses she oversees at Black Diamond Ranch are both ranked among Florida's top ten.

Sexism has never been an issue, says Laurie, "probably because I've worked my way up. I started out in the trenches. When they see you down there in a hole full of mud, it kind of takes the male-female thing out of it."

The fact that she came up through the ranks also makes it possible for her to successfully manage a work force that averages sixty people. "Nothing," says Laurie, "no matter what you do in college, prepares you for management. But you will never hear me say, 'That person works for me.' It's always, 'That person works with me.'"

And if that's not always literally true – "I can't be out there doing it like I used to" – Laurie wishes that it were. She's just not the sit-behind-the-desk type. "I'm not a real good office work person. Anybody can tell you that. I spend maybe 20 percent of my time in the office.

Her favorite part of the job? "Mowing the fairways. You get on that machine, nobody bothers you. Fresh-cut grass – there's nothing better. And looking back when you're done and seeing those straight-lined stripes. To me that's special."

Along the way, Laurie has come to enjoy picking up a golf club every now and then. "I'm a bogey golfer," she says. "I can drive and I can putt. It's just that part in the middle I haven't figured out yet."

She will, though, because she's not going anywhere. "I wouldn't trade places with anybody in the world right now. Hopefully, I'll be here for a long time."

Ed Grant

PAST PRESIDENT, THE THUNDERBIRDS
THE SANTA CLAUS GOLF CLASSIC
TPC SCOTTSDALE, SCOTTSDALE, ARIZONA

"Honey, 'Guess what?' I just won the car."

Virtue is its own reward. But if you want to throw in a new car as a bonus, Ed Grant won't say no.

For years Ed has served as a mainstay of the Thunderbirds, a special projects committee of the Phoenix Chamber of Commerce. "Our mission is to promote Phoenix through sports," he explains, and the group's biggest undertaking, year in and year out, is its sponsorship of the Phoenix Open.

Ed was president of the Thunderbirds in 1996 and 1997 and also served as tournament chairman in 1996. With considerable pride he claims for the 65-year-old Phoenix Open the title of "the largest spectated golf tournament in the world."

In conjunction with the Open, the Thunderbirds each year put on the Santa Claus Classic, the celebrity pro-am event preceding the tournament. Ed calls this super-successful fundraiser "one of the more exclusive pro-ams in the country" and quickly gives credit to the local tour stars – especially Andrew McGee and Gary McCord – who generously sacrifice their time and effort to make it work.

"In a lot of these pro-ams," says Ed, "the pros are there because they have to be there. . . But in ours, the pros are there because they want to be, and they treat the people that way. So any time you play in the Santa Claus Classic, you're going to have a good time."

Ed's involvement has been a labor of love – ordained by fate. During his college years, Ed caddied for a touring pro named Fred Marty, and during one Christmas holiday season, Ed got the call to come to Pebble Beach. He drove 16 hours straight from Tucson to California and worked the week for Fred and his amateur partner, a man named Bob Goldwater. The $250-dollar tip from Mr. Goldwater was memorable enough, but the connection Ed cherishes is that Bob Goldwater turned out to be the so-called "Father of the Phoenix Open," the founder and ten-time chairman of the tournament. "After all these years," says Ed, "to end up being chairman of that same event, that's very ironic and quite an honor."

Oh yeah, about that car. It seems that this year, free of official responsibilities, Ed fired "closest to the pin" in the Santa Claus Shoot-Out and took home a new Buick LeSabre Sport.

Let Ed describe the action: You've got Gary McCord on the mike trying to give you a hard time, talking to you about shanking the ball. I was so nervous. I just hoped I wouldn't lay the sod over the top of the ball right there in front of everybody."

Given Ed's years of service, nobody could have hoped for a more deserving winner.

Chuck Jonas

SALESMAN, GOLF GALAXY
MINNEAPOLIS, MINNESOTA

"If you want to stay healthy, play a lot of golf and walk every step."

Eighty-seven-year-old Chuck Jonas attributes his longevity not simply to playing golf but to playing golf on foot – which he has done for 78 years. "I've walked every step of the way, and I still walk," Chuck insists. "People who ride carts are not avid golfers."

Chuck began walking golf courses at the age of nine in Titusville, Pennsylvania. He decided to start caddying at the local course to earn a few nickels each day, so he approached the caddy master. "The guy was about 18 years old. His name was Gene Sarazen. Seven years later he won the Masters. Isn't that a beautiful thing – from caddy master to Masters champion."

Chuck calls that first experience "a wonderful way to get into the game." The stories he tells make it obvious that he never had any inclination to get back out. He vividly remembers the time Walter Hagan came to Chicago to put on an exhibition. "He arrived in a Cadillac about six o'clock Saturday night, went right to the bar and never left. When I came back in the morning to see the exhibition, Walter could barely wobble out of the clubhouse. I'm thinking, how can he be enjoyable to watch when he's that far gone? Well, he just came out quietly and broke the course record."

Ben Hogan was Chuck's favorite, though, and he was sure to be in the gallery whenever Hogan came to Chicago. "Ben's only words during the entire 18 holes would be, 'You're away,'" recalls Chuck. "They say that his mother could be having a heart attack in the middle of the fairway, and Ben would calmly step over her and keep going. He was wonderful to watch."

Caddying at a club close to Chicago's downtown, it's not surprising that Chuck got to know various members of "the syndicate." Al Capone's brother Ralph played regularly one summer, without ever bothering to call for a tee-time. Instead, Ralph and his girlfriend would show up, and Ralph's bodyguard would ask Chuck to get them on. "I'm booked. I'm solid," remembers Chuck, "but I'm going to get the Capone boy on, no matter what."

After their last round that season, Billy Showers, the bodyguard, approached Chuck to express Ralph's gratitude. "At that time," says Chuck, "there's not much money in the world, so I'm thinking maybe he'll give me twenty dollars." He asked Billy what Ralph had in mind, and Billy replied, "Ralph told me to tell you, if you ever want anybody taken out, we'll take care of it. Nobody'll ever know."

Chuck says the offer didn't do him much good since he was friends with everybody he knew. Then he adds, "If only I could find that guy now."

Bill Mayfair

PGA Tour Player
The Santa Claus Classic
TPC Scottsdale
Scottsdale, Arizona

". . . golf is all about competition. I just love competing against the best players in the world week after week."

It made perfect sense to Billy Mayfair to get married on the 18th green at TPC at Las Colinas prior to the 1994 Byron Nelson Classic. "After all," he says, "we knew we were going to be spending the rest of our lives on golf courses, so we thought we might as well get married on one."

The timing proved right as well. The year before, Billy had won his first PGA Tour event, the 1993 Greater Milwaukee Open, and the following year – confirming the marriage as a good omen – he won twice, the Western Open and The Tour Championship.

Actually, Billy has been living on golf courses since the age of five, when his father cut down and regripped some clubs for the future PGA Tour star. But Billy says it was during his college days at Arizona State that he came to realize he had both the potential and the desire to take a crack at the tour. It's no wonder. He won the Fred Haskins Award as the nation's top collegiate player, along with the 1986 U.S. Public Links and the 1987 U.S. Amateur titles.

Billy's 12 years on the tour continue to bear witness to the potential and the desire. In 1998, he again won twice – the Nissan Open and the Buick Open – bringing his trophy total to five, and he's also had a half-dozen second-place finishes.

The desire doesn't seem to be waning, either. "For me," says Billy, "golf is all about competition. I just love competing against the best players in the world week after week."

But regardless of the level you play at, according to Billy, golf is the "common ground" that can facilitate whatever you want to do. "Playing golf puts you on equal terms with CEOs and presidents and anyone else in the world. Because just about everybody plays golf. Golf doesn't have to be your career for it to be a great part of your life."

You can even get married on the golf course, which Billy might recommend: "That wedding and the birth of my son, Maxwell, are two of the greatest experiences of my life."

Jones Family, Three Generations

SWEETWATER COUNTRY CLUB
LONGWOOD, FLORIDA

"I've learned from golf that the quick, expedient way is really the wrong way – with no way back home." (Jeff Jones)

The Jones family golfing saga has its origins in Nashville, Tennessee, when Bill – now the patriarch – was a kid living near a public course. "I started out caddying," says Bill, "back when they had those big old leather bags. We'd carry doubles, caddy all day, and think we were rich when we went home with three or four dollars."

Bill fell in love with the game, he says, and "played a lot of golf" up until he joined the navy during the Korean War. He had pretty much put the clubs away, but when his sons, Jeff and Rusty, started playing in high school, the clubs came back out." What's more," says Bill, "My wife didn't want to be a golf widow, so she began playing, too, and got more addicted than any of us."

Jeff, now the head pro at Sweetwater, picks up the story: "I was one of those kids who grow up playing every sport except golf. But when I found myself entering ninth grade weighing about 80 pounds, my options were limited." He discovered golf – a sport where size and physical strength didn't matter much – and never looked back. "I got my brother interested," he says, "and we spent every day that summer – 10, 12, 14, hours a day – at the golf course."

If it hadn't been already, his fate was sealed the day he went to watch the Jerry Ford invitational in Vail. "This was in 1973," he says, "when Jack Nicklaus was really in his prime. On the back nine there's a par-three with an elevated tee. My friend and I snuck through the ropes and went up there, and there was no other gallery around. So we're standing there waiting, and we hear these spikes coming up the cart path, and lo and behold, there comes Jack Nicklaus and his caddy. I mean, we thought we had witnessed the second coming."

Growing up in Colorado and playing seasonally, Jeff couldn't wait to move to Arizona, where he could play 365 days a year and work his way on to the tour. But what he found in Arizona was "literally hundreds and thousands of awesome golfers," nudging him toward the transition to the teaching side of professional golf.

Where, as it happens, he has been quite happy. Even as a head pro, he still gives twenty or thirty lessons a week. "I'm not one to be confined to an office," he says. "Outside, interacting with the people is the place I belong."

Meanwhile, the third generation is coming along, represented by Taylor and Trevor, and, more recently, Spencer. As Grandfather Bill puts it, "Jeff has produced a built-in foursome for himself."

Dick Horton

EXECUTIVE DIRECTOR, TENNESSEE SECTION PGA , AND TENNESSEE GOLF ASSOCIATION
PRESIDENT, TENNESSEE GOLF FOUNDATION
TENNESSEE GOLF HOUSE

"I don't want to say that golf people are fanatical because every sport has its fanatics. But how about the guy who goes out there and shoots 120 and can't wait to get back out there the next day? What does that tell you?"

At age 22, right out of Wake Forest, Dick Horton became the first executive director of the Tennessee Section PGA.

"An interesting story," says Dick. "When I came to the interview, we had a pretty feisty debate over whether the job would be full- or part-time. Finally they said that whoever they hired could call it whatever he wanted, but the salary was $7,000. They also said that they had $3,500 in the bank, so if it was a full-time job then the person who took it would have to spend the first half of the year raising the money to be able to pay himself for the second half." The original office was in his apartment, with furnishings discarded from local country clubs.

Now, he says, between the three associations – including also the Tennessee Golf Association and the Tennessee Golf Foundation – "we probably have around $8 million in assets."

Thanks largely to Dick's leadership of both the Tennessee Section PGA (the professional body) and the Tennessee Golf Association (the amateur body), Tennessee has managed what many states have not: "In many states the professionals and amateurs are at cross-purposes, competing with each other. But here, for a long time now, the professionals, the amateurs, the women, the juniors have all come together with the common purpose of making golf in Tennessee a better game."

More specifically, out of the cooperation between the two bodies has come the Tennessee Golf Foundation, the charitable foundation through which has been created Golf House of Tennessee, the Tennessee Golf Hall of Fame, and a variety of successful youth programs.

"Our mission is really pretty simple," says Dick. "We're trying to grow the game. If you grow the game, every single facet of it benefits. There are no losers."

The numbers say Dick has been successful. In 1973 the association was involved in three major junior tournaments. Now, during a 53-day summer season, there are 152 events for the 1,400 boy and girl members. In 1973, the association handicapped 6,000 amateur golfers in the state. That number today is 42,000. Dick is also quick to point out that David Gossett of Memphis, the reigning U.S. Amateur champ, and Danny Green from Jackson, the USGA Mid-Amateur champion, are graduates of his association's junior program.

"We don't get a lot of notoriety as a golf state," says Dick, "but golf is a wonderfully successful sport here in Tennessee."

Evan Byers

PRINCIPAL, BYERS WEST GROUP
RIVIERA COUNTRY CLUB
LOS ANGELES, CALIFORNIA

"One day an interviewer asked Mr. Callaway why, at age 74, he still came in to the office at 7:30 every morning? 'Son,' he said, 'my name is on the door.' That was all he said. That was enough."

Where would Big Bertha be today if Evan Byers hadn't broken his leg for the third time at age 17, bringing his career as a downhill ski racer to an untimely end?

The broken leg consigned him to the golf course in Steamboat Springs, where he worked retrieving range balls, and, he says, "actually started hitting balls with the cast still on his leg."

Golf quickly became Evan's focus, and, once he realized he had "neither the financial backing nor the game to compete," he got into the business as an assistant pro and spent a few years working the Colorado resort towns. He turned next to caddying and soon found himself carrying the bags of Orville Moody and Larry Mowry on the Senior Tour. Despite considerable success – he was on Mowry's bag when he won the Senior PGA – two years was long enough.

Contemplating what to do next, he got a call from E. B. Callaway, founder of Callaway Golf. "We had met before, and he wanted me to come look at his product lines. He asked me how they could get the tour players to use their clubs, and when I came up with a plan, they hired me to do it. I was called Tour Representative, their very first tour rep. That was

twelve years ago, the beginning of Callaway's big run."

Success didn't come overnight. "I took the clubs out to the tour and people just laughed at me," says Evan. But player by player, he began to win them over. "The players knew me," he says, "and I was very careful of my reputation and of my relationship with these guys."

Soon Evan began watching the Darrell Survey, which keeps track of every piece of equipment that every player uses. "I would sit with the Darrell people, watch all the players tee off, and we'd count how many drivers Callaway had." Taylor-made was #1, says Evan; they were the target.

"We went from nothing to about, like, 40 players using the driver – 35 to 40 percent of the field – and that made us #1. I remember the day it happened. I ran to call the office and told Mr. Callaway, 'You're #1. We finally beat Taylor-made.' From the time I started, it took about three years to become #1 on the PGA Tour."

Now Evan runs his own company, Byers West Group, representing a wide variety of golf manufacturers to the PGA Tour, and tries his best to raise a family. He may have a prodigy on his hands. "My three-year-old spends about an hour a day hitting golf balls. And I'm not Earl Woods! It's awesome."

Gail Liniger

CEO, RE/MAX
SANCTUARY GOLF CLUB
SEDALIA, COLORADO

"It's so hard to be consistent from one day to the next, but the good rounds keep you coming back."

It is remarkable enough that Gail Liniger is the cofounder and CEO of a multinational corporation with 3400 offices in 34 countries. It may be even more remarkable that, even after losing the use of one arm in a seaplane accident, Gail decided to take up golf.

"We live on a golf course," she explains, "and we always walked the course for exercise, so it seemed like a good idea." The club pro encouraged her. "He said he thought I could play with one arm, and after I took a lesson I decided, yes, I would go for it."

On second thought, maybe it's not so remarkable. After all, golf is golf – its pleasures, its frustrations, its mysteries – and Gail's accident in no way limits her experience of this most alluring game.

"First of all, I love just being outdoors," says Gail, "and there are beautiful golf courses all around us just to see. But beyond that there's the challenge of just trying to get better, trying to improve my game."

Then, too, there is the wonderful release from the worrisome, un-golf world that occupies most of our waking moments. "I just forget about everything at the office," says Gail, "and concentrate on the golf. It's wonderful relaxation and stress relief."

And, of course, golf is a stern and undiscriminating taskmaster: it teaches the same hard lessons to all comers. "It's just like anything else you do," says Gail. "If you want to get better, you work at it. You practice. I can't just stand up there and give a presentation to a group of RE/MAX associates without doing the work first."

Lesson two: When you hit it bad, move on. "You can't let one shot affect the rest of your round," declares Gail. "Each hole is a new hole."

Ken Venturi never spoke truer words.

Bill Kidd

Head Golf Professional, Retired
Interlochen Country Club
Minneapolis, Minnesota

"I went to work for my dad in 1953. We had a nice association. In fact, he taught me everything I know."

For 35 years, from 1958 to 1993, Bill Kidd served as head pro at Interlochen Country Club in Minneapolis. The only other man to enjoy such long tenure there happened to be Bill's father, who was head pro from 1920 until Bill took over. The two careers add up to 73 years on the same golf course.

"Yeah, it was a nice run," Bill observes.

After his long lifetime in the sport, Bill says that the thing that still amazes him is that golf is so unpredictable. "You can just be playing along, thinking you've got everything under control, and – bingo! – out of nowhere something'll just pop up."

That's what sets the touring pros apart, Bill believes. "Sure, they've got the touch and feel, but the amazing thing is that they can concentrate for 72 holes. I might be able to hold it together for maybe four or five holes."

An avowed traditionalist, Bill glances with a wary eye at the extremes to which golf course construction has gone in recent years, "now that they have all this equipment to move heaven and earth." He cites as an example a course in Palm Springs that cost $54 million to build. "I guarantee you," he says, "Pebble Beach didn't cost $54,000 to build. To tell you the truth, I prefer what God made to what man made."

Like Interlochen, one of the "good old courses,"

on which Bill has collected his storehouse of memories. He recalls the time the Open was being played at Hazeltine; a heavy rain washed out one of the rounds, and Gary Player called to see if he could come over and play a round with Bill.

"By the sixth hole we had a pretty good gallery," says Bill. "Every time Gary would go into a bunker, he'd hit three balls out, and two of the three would go right in the hole – just about every time. Unbelievable sand player." Bill also admits that Gary was "a little bit different," by virtue of his obsession with physical fitness. "We have some big hills out there, and Gary would run up those hills backwards – said it was good for the back of your legs. Of course, he's still playing well today."

Bill also had a memorable round with Mark Calcavecchia. "He was on his way back to England to defend his British Open title when we played. We have five par-5s, three of them pretty good size, and he hit every one in two. He shot the easiest 68 I ever saw." Meanwhile, Bill's own game is holding up. He's already shot his age – 72 – and he recently won the Half-Century Championship (a tournament for those who have been PGA members for 50 years or more). But he's modest about the achievement: "There aren't too many guys around who qualify to get in that field."

Jim Plunkett

RETIRED OAKLAND RAIDER QUARTERBACK
STANFORD UNIVERSITY GOLF COURSE
STANFORD, CALIFORNIA

"I used to lose my temper, throw my clubs. Finally I've learned that there's nothing less important than your last shot."

Two-time Super Bowl winner Jim Plunkett speaks eloquently on behalf of the many world-class athletes who seek to unravel the mysteries of golf. Of necessity, he began to take the game seriously early in his NFL career.

"As a pro football player," says Jim, "I would get invited to all these charity golf events. I didn't like embarrassing myself so I made an effort to learn the game." He was quickly hooked by the challenge. "All athletes are competitive. So all of a sudden you not only want to play, you want to play well. Then you find out it's not as easy as it looks."

Like so many athletes from other sports, Jim has been forced to conclude that "Golf is a different game. Period." Throwing the football had become second nature to him, he says, and for that particular athletic task he had developed "muscle memory." But even though over the years he has hit thousands of golf balls, says Jim, "I still don't really have a grooved swing. It can still change from day to day."

In fact, Jim believes that golf is perhaps the one sport where natural ability doesn't cut it. "Football, basketball, baseball – you can go out there and do a lot with your athletic ability. What's different about golf is that you really have to get some instruction if you want to get good at it. A golf pro can see things that you cannot see or feel."

But Jim is also keenly appreciative of the special rewards golf offers: "On the golf course I'm away from my phone, mail, concrete, smog, automobiles. I'm out where it's green and beautiful. I can forget all my troubles. I played Pebble Beach the other day, and, out there, I play the worst golf of my life and still have one of my best days ever."

Jim acknowledges that "there's no feeling in the world" like hitting that one great shot, but also the generosity of spirit that golf fosters: "The thing is, you're out there playing with other people, and when they hit a good golf shot, you feel good for them, too."

For Jim, the power of the game's appeal was best illustrated the day he played with a man who had cerebral palsy. "He'd swing, lose his balance, and because of his affliction, would fall flat on his face. He didn't care. He wasn't about to give up golf."

Karen Bednarsky

Director, World Golf Hall of Fame
St. Augustine, Florida

"When you think about the members of the Hall of Fame, they're people of character, dedication, passion, and discipline. I hope that when people come here they think about those qualities."

With a background in art and photography, a love of golf, and a hankering for a new career, Karen Bednarsky answered an ad in the paper.

After working in "almost every department at the USGA," Karen found herself working for Janet Seigel, the longtime curator of the USGA Museum and Library. "Virtually everything was in her head," says Karen. "No data bases, no books, no manuscripts, nothing on paper, so I was in effect Janet's understudy for three years."

Upon Janet's retirement, Karen stayed on as curator for seven years, then got the call from the newly developing World Golf Hall of Fame. "The idea of being involved from the ground up was very tempting," she says. "I arrived about eighteen months before we were open and had the opportunity to play a real role in creating the exhibit experience we have here."

Under Karen's directorship, that experience combines the richest of golf's history and traditions with the latest in interactive technology. "We really wanted people to be able to immerse themselves in the environment of golf," says Karen.

Perhaps the most enjoyable exhibit, according to Karen, is the swing analyzer, "where you get to hit three golf balls and get some feedback on your accuracy, distance, and tempo." What makes this exhibit particularly unique, though, is that the results are linked to a data base of golf pros' swings, so that you get to find out which player your swing is most like. "People really love that," says Karen. "Everybody always gets linked with somebody."

The mission of the World Golf Hall of Fame, says Karen, is to broaden the audience for the game of golf, and at the same time to put on display the best qualities of golf's greatest players. "If people can find someone here who accomplished something that inspires them to be more or do more in their own lives, then I think we've really hit the mark."

The idea of touching the lives of children has special appeal, and Karen sees this happening – especially in connection with the exploding fame of Tiger Woods. "The school kids that come here are often asked to draw pictures of their visit, and I sometimes have pictures come back with just the Nike logo on them. Nowhere in the Hall of Fame is there a Nike logo, but it symbolizes Tiger Woods! I think that says great things about the impact of the game of golf."

Notah Begay III

PGA TOUR PLAYER
RIVIERA COUNTRY CLUB
LOS ANGELES, CALIFORNIA

"My career on the PGA Tour is a testament to the fact that it doesn't matter where you come from – only where you go."

When Notah Begay III won twice on the PGA Tour in 1999, the golf media had found a story. It wasn't just that Notah was a tour rookie, winning more titles in his inaugural season than many tour veterans do in their careers. Even more unusual was that Notah, who grew up on the Isleta Pueblo Reservation near Albuquerque, is believed to be the first full-blooded Native American to appear on the Tour.

Notah acknowledges right away that he didn't come from a typical golfer's background, but the scant exposure to golf available to him was sufficient. At age six he was following behind as his father played league golf in Albuquerque, and soon thereafter he was spending summers shagging balls and cleaning carts in exchange for the chance to hit range balls during every spare moment.

By the end of his high school years, his game was such that colleges were interested. He ultimately won a scholarship to Stanford, where his teammates were Tiger Woods and Casey Martin, among others. Notah more than held his own, becoming a three-time All-American, and firing an NCAA-record 62 to help the team take the '94 national championship.

When he followed that up with a 59 on the Nike Tour a couple of years later, it became apparent that Notah is one of those golfers who likes to aim low. "I don't get scared," he says. "We [pros] play so much golf that when we're really on, we should be able to shoot 60, not 65."

The two victories in '99, along with the more than $1.2 million in prize money, would in almost any other year have made Notah a shoe-in for Rookie of the Year. Though he lost that honor to Carlos Franco, another two-time winner, the successful year landed him squarely in celebrity's spotlight.

For Notah, that means opportunity – to break down barriers and shatter stereotypes. He relishes the chance to be a spokesman for the Native American community – and to be a role model for Native American youngsters.

"I'm pursuing that opportunity," he says. "I really do want to influence and inspire kids. Historically golf has been a privileged sport, but I never let that get in the way of my dream. My message to kids is: Work hard and follow your dreams!"

Roger Maltbie

NBC Golf Analyst and former PGA Tour player
Doral Ryder Open, Miami, Florida

"The unique thing about golf is that it has the very same power over both the expert and the amateur. No one is ever going to master the game, but anyone, at any moment, might strike a solid, perfect golf shot. It's that feeling that brings you back."

As a longtime PGA Tour player and a now veteran NBC golf analyst, Roger Maltbie has taken a close look at the game. As a man in his late 40s with the Senior Tour looming, he's still looking.

And he isn't deluded by what he sees: "I think these seniors sometimes get a little off-kilter saying they're playing the best golf of their lives. I mean, they're playing shorter courses, with less rough. The courses are set up to be much less difficult. The competition is not nearly as deep. If these guys 'playing the best golf of their lives' tried to return to the PGA Tour, they'd have no success. That's just the way it is."

But this self-styled "old coot" has tremendous respect not only for the old players but for the old days of golf. "These kids now," he says, "they've got their swing coaches, sports psychologists, professionals that travel with them all the time. They have club repair facilities on the grounds. Used to be, if you needed a lesson you went home."

Now pro golf is big business, "and your entertainment comes from watching the best players making great shots. Rightfully so," says Roger, who harbors no grudge. But he admits to a certain nostalgia for the "characters" of years past – Doug Sanders,

Dutch Harrison and their ilk. "Back then golf was a traveling road show. It wasn't that many years ago that the pros weren't even allowed in the clubhouse. They were viewed as nomads, rogues, vagabonds, hustlers. That's what they did. They could make more money gambling on the side with club members than they could if they won the tournament.

"On the other hand, the essence of the game – its utterly unique character – hasn't changed. "Golf's sense of sportsmanship and fair play, for instance," says Roger, "is unparalleled. If you can hold in football and get away with it, that's good. If a pitcher can load up the baseball and get away with it, that's good. Golf is not a game where it's okay to break the rules."

Roger also has a theory about the absence of drug use in golf. "Golf is not about trying to get faster, or bigger, or tougher, or more pumped up. Golf is all about quieting the mind, removing all extraneous thoughts. They haven't made a drug that would help you play golf."

And then, amid all the frustrations that all golfers suffer, there comes that moment of grace: "You'll never know," says Roger, "what it's like to stand behind center in a Super Bowl. You'll never know what it's like to be Joe Montana, say. But you can, for one brief moment, know what it's like to feel like Tiger Woods."

Stan Olsen

OWNER/DEVELOPER, BLACK DIAMOND RANCH
BLACK DIAMOND RANCH, FLORIDA

"There are other designers, especially here in Florida, who have a difficult time working with the flatlands. So they drop Hershey Kisses here and there. It creates an interesting effect but it doesn't feel natural at all."

Stan Olsen, who helped build Digital Equipment Corporation from a company of three into a powerhouse of 95,000, has found a second career building golf course developments. Not really such a stretch, says Stan, given the fact that he has always been a systems engineer, specializing in "putting it all together," and a golf community is a "total system."

He has also had some help, he admits, in the shaping of his vision as a developer. He gives great credit to his son, wildlife photographer John Olsen. "I can go out in the woods with him and learn more about trees, wildlife, and nature in a half-hour than I could in an entire semester in school," says Stan, whose own appreciation of nature is an essential component of his vision as a developer.

Stan has also come to be an adherent of the Oriental philosophy of feng shui, which, he says, defines straight lines as "poison arrows that affect not only your vision but also your well-being and mentality." The object, then, is to "remove the poison arrows from the environment, locate things in the right places, and you'll have health, happiness, and good fortune." On the golf course, more specifically, you'll have "a natural, calming, beautiful experience."

Of course, in a golf development, which by definition includes houses "with all these straight lines," the worthy goals of feng shui are difficult to attain. Stan's solution is "to put the built environment into the background and draw the natural environment into the foreground."

Trees, by nature "beautiful and calming, with their flowing effect," are a critical component of the course landscape. Not only salutary in themselves, they also obscure the rooflines of the houses, which constitute "an interference." "You want to be able to concentrate on your game, on getting the distance right, on hitting straight to your target," Stan says, "without being interfered with. It's the natural plants and trees that give you the feeling you want."

But, ultimately, Stan's mission isn't that complicated: "I want every member to have the best day every day."

146

Al Cornish, Mark Bowman & Tom Boots

THE PELICAN BEACH SHOOT-OUT
HYANNIS, NEBRASKA

"I told Pat Hammert, who was playing ahead of us, 'If you're hitting golf shots that good, your cows must look like hell.'" (Mark Bowman)

First imagine a tiny ranching community in Nebraska with only 210 residents. Then imagine such a town deciding to build a golf club. If you can get that far, you'll have no trouble conceiving of the Pelican Beach Shoot-Out.

Jeanne Davis, as secretary-treasurer, has been running the event since its inception in 1995, and if anybody can explain it, she can.

Her husband, she says, was one of the men in town who had the idea of creating the Pelican Beach Golf Club, which would consist, to begin with, of three holes. "We knew we would have to figure out a way to fund the thing, and our president came up with the idea of a fundraiser that would combine some of the activities we do in this area. In addition to golf, we would have trap-shooting and calf-roping."

This year, the event drew 23 three-man teams, some of which traveled more than 100 miles to participate.

Three-year veteran Al Cornish, from Alliance, 60 miles away, describes the format: "You shoot a round of trap, then you go out and play golf, then the two who are the better ropers go rope a steer or two and the other guy goes and plays golf. I'm the so-called

golfer in our group, and those other guys [teammates Mark Bowman and Tom Boots] are really good ropers, so that's how we divide up."

Al says his teammates "don't get too serious" about the golf. Which is a good thing. As Mark explains, his participation in Shoot-Out constitutes his entire experience with the game. After all, at the

148

Pelican Beach Shoot-Out, playing good golf is hardly the point. "It's all about the camaraderie, friends just getting together and catching up with our news, laughing at each other and ourselves." In fact, says Mark, if one of his friends starts looking good on the golf course, there must be trouble back on the ranch. "I told Pat Hammert, who was playing ahead of us, 'If you're hitting golf shots that good, your cows must look like hell.'

Even Al, a good player who admits that he does get a little too serious about the golf part, can see the bigger picture. "Anybody who was wondering whether or not to come to Pelican Beach, I'd tell him, 'You're going to have a hell of a good time. You're going to meet some nice people – I mean, nice people. You might not win, but you're going to have a good time.'"

In the meantime, the three-hole golf course now has nine holes, with 40 family and 15 individual memberships, and Hyannis has a lot of pride in its accomplishment. "It was just all volunteers," says Jeanne, "with local businesses donating equipment – the sprinkler system, the plastic pipe – and volunteers doing all the work, the planting and digging."

Jeanne looks forward to the day when the club has its own building, so that the golf carts, for instance, won't have to borrow fairground space from the 4-H and other groups. But for now, it's amazing to think that, thanks to the Pelican Beach Shoot-Out, Hyannis, Nebraska, has a nine-hole golf course with irrigated fairways and automatic sprinklers on every green.

In fact, says Jeanne, the entire project – the golf club and the fundraiser that supports it – was named one of the state's top ten rural economic development initiatives – complete with an award ceremony at the state capitol.

"We really thought that was neat," admits Jeanne.

Mike Schussman

Foursome Member
Stanford University Golf Course
Stanford, California

"We have guys in our club who shoot their age quite often. I'll do it when I get to be a hundred."

Mike Schussman has been playing golf long enough to have learned how to maximize the pleasures of the sport and minimize its agonies.

"I can describe my experience of golf as a gradual relaxation. When I first started playing, of course, I was worried about how I did, worried about my technique, worried about having a bad shot, so golf was very frustrating. Half the time, you'd end up cussing."

Sometimes years do bring wisdom. "Gradually I began to realize, 'Hey, if I play the best I can, that's all I can do. If I miss a shot, so what – I'm not perfect.' So over the years my golf game has become more fun and less strain." But that's not all, Mike adds. "The truth is, I'm playing a better game of golf now than I did 20 years ago. If anything, my handicap has gone down a little bit."

Mike, it should be noted, is 82. He's been playing the course at Stanford for more than 30 years – and with the same foursome for about 10 years. The lessons he's learned are part of the group's communal experience. "Most of our older guys figure they're lucky just to be out there. They're not going to worry too much about missing a putt."

A career teacher and administrator in the San Mateo County public schools, Mike likes what golf can teach kids about individual challenge and individual responsibility: "Golf is not a team sport, where you depend on other people, whether teammates or referees. It's a game where you depend on yourself, and also a game that rewards you individually. The bottom line is: you are just as good or bad as you make yourself."

At the same time, especially among his golfing peers, Mike keenly appreciates the social aspect of the game. "For us," he says, "it's all camaraderie, community, and day-to-day bantering. Being out there together playing the game is much more important to us than winning."

Mike and his foursome play in a seniors league that includes exchanges with other clubs and even dinners together. "Strictly a social deal," he says, but he realizes that the way the social and individual aspects of the game intertwine is part of golf's magic.

"You see, it's each individual on his own on the golf course, but you go through these experiences out there – I'm thinking of the bad ones – and eventually you realize, 'Hey, everybody else has done these same things.' It really creates a common bond. Golfers know how to empathize."

Roger Maxwell

PROPRIETOR, IN CELEBRATION OF GOLF
SCOTTSDALE, ARIZONA

"If you have integrity in the game of golf, you'll have integrity in the rest of your life."

Roger Maxwell's life in golf followed a more or less conventional path until he reached the age of fifty: caddying at the municipal course in Oklahoma City as a boy; working his way up to first assistant at the club while developing his playing skills; attending Oklahoma State on a golf scholarship; going to work for the Marriot Corporation and eventually becoming vice president in charge of all of Marriot's golf operations.

"Then I retired from Marriot," Roger says, "in order to pursue my own dream, which was to create a concept like nothing that had ever been seen before."

The dream came true, and Roger called it In Celebration of Golf – a golfing retail store that would make even the most confirmed shopaphobic browse in wonder and delight. "Our goal was to bring together all of the romance, all of the history and tradition of the game at the retail level. To our knowledge, no one else has ever done this."

Don't come to In Celebration of Golf for your Xed-out Titleists, your whiffle balls, or any of your golf gimmicks and gags. On the other hand, you will find beautiful statuary, rare and antique books, hand-carved bookends, custom crafted golf furniture, not to mention the finest in clubs, shoes, and clothing.

Take Roger's golf bags, for example: "We don't buy any golf bags out of a catalog; they are all hand-made for us. We choose fabrics from around the world and have the bags made specially for this store."

And then there's the golf cart, purchased from the El Dorado Country Club, from the very first fleet of carts they had back in the early fifties. "Very, very likely," says Roger, "that Ike Eisenhower rode on this golf cart."

Roger loves the history of the game, and he hoped to bring an attitude of respect to the retail end. "Off-course retailing had never been reflective of the true spirit of the game, its tremendous history, and that's what we wanted to create with In Celebration of Golf."

Roger's family has added to that history. When he was still a 12-year-old caddy, a horse belonging to his 15-year-old sister, Suzie, got loose and ran onto the nearby golf course. Chasing it down on her other horse, Suzie did $600 worth of damage to one of the greens. Her parents demanded that she sell the horses to pay for the damage, which, tearfully, she did. When she took the money to the fabled club professional there, U. C. Ferguson Jr., he gave her a set of golf clubs, welcomed her to play there, and even offered her lessons. "She had never picked up a golf club in her life," says Roger, "but ten years later Suzie won her first U.S. Open and went on to win two more."

Something to celebrate.

Mayor's Cup Champions

River Valley Ranch
Carbondale, Colorado

Bobbie and J. T. Thompson, Larry Ledingham, and Larry Lederer, along with a "designated ringer," have been teaming up at the annual Aspen Mayor's Cup for the last eight years. For the last two years in a row (last year with Eri Crum and this year with Jimmy Rodriguez), they've taken home the championship.

During the victory celebration, the players were prevailed upon to explain what draws them back to the scramble-format event year after year. J.T., who says he plays in every local tournament at the Aspen course, just loves to compete: "I just like to play competitively, and this is a great combination of fun and competition. There's not a lot of pressure, and the format makes for a lot of camaraderie and a really fun day." His wife, Bobbi, doesn't entirely agree: "I certainly don't do it for the competition, but every summer I look forward to this. It's my favorite day of the summer. It's just so much fun cheering for each other." Bobbi also finds a pleasurable irony in finding her team in the winner's circle: "We are really a motley group. I mean, nobody would put their money on us. But in this format, even the bozos get to be champions on any given day."

Larry Ledingham offers a unique perspective on the event: "It gives me an excuse to clean my golf clubs once a summer." But he's quick to put his finger on the special appeal of the scramble format: "The thing is, we all get to be a hero — at least once during the day." His own experience a few hours earlier bore out the observation. He skulled his second shot on the par-4 first hole, and the team watched in dismay as it skimmed along the ground 180 yards, rolled up onto the green and into the cup. Eagle!

For Larry Lederer, not the lowest handicapper on the team, the pleasure is elemental: "The thing I like best is that I never get to put that many birdies and eagles on the scorecard. Somebody asks, 'How'd you do?' and you say, 'Oh, we were 14 under.' That's just great."

Last year's ringer, Eri, loves the rare opportunity to violate one of the game's fundamental rules: "It's great to have the freedom to get up there and swing as hard as you can. And if you miss, you pick it up and play somebody else's ball." There is a catch, though: "The problem is, you get done playing a scramble and go out the next day and you're swinging about thirty times faster."

Jimmy, this year's ringer, has transformed himself from a 27-handicapper into a 2, and he enjoys the rewards of that hard labor: "It's fun to have gotten to this level, when maybe nobody's hit the green and they're looking at me . . . . to know that you can do it, bring home the bacon, be the Mark McGuire or Sammy Sosa stepping to the plate. To be the guy that maybe makes the shot to keep us in it."

More philosophically, he adds, "Also, this is one of the few times in golf that you get to play with a team. Golf is such an 'I' sport, but for one day it becomes a team sport. I think you miss out on that as you get older."

Al Mengert

RETIRED DIRECTOR OF GOLF
LEGEND TRAIL
SCOTTSDALE, ARIZONA

"Tommy Armour once said, 'The halo of fame sometimes clouds our memory.' I love that line because I've seen people who let their accomplishments change their personality."

Looks like a good life, doesn't it? Million dollar purses, lucrative endorsements, private jets to whisk us from one green and blue paradise to the next.

Well, things have changed. Fifty years ago, the now-vaunted PGA Tour offered a life that the best player in the world might just respectfully decline.

In 1952, after winning the Mexican Amateur and the Northwest Open and being runner-up in the U.S. Amateur, Al Mengert was the #1-ranked amateur in the country. The pro tour beckoned. "I thought about it, sure," says Al. "If I continued to improve, there wasn't any reason I couldn't be one of the top pros."

But Al already had a wife and a child and, more important, an invitation to go to work for Claude Harmon at Winged Foot. That offer, for Al, was more attractive than the vagaries of the touring life. Two incidents convinced him he'd made the right choice. First, while Harmon was still at Seminole, where he worked during the winter, Al was opening the mail and saw a check to Harmon for $25,000. "I thought, 'My gosh, $25,000 – he'd have to win twelve tournaments to get this much money, and he hasn't even come to work yet.'"

The second occurred when Ben Hogan came to play an exhibition at Winged Foot and asked Al to come to Palm Springs in the winter and assist him at Tamarisk Country Club. "So I'm thinking about Harmon's check for $25,000 and Ben Hogan taking a club job after winning three majors in one year . . . well, that made an impression on me. Club life was the way to go."

One benefit of club life, according to Al's daughter Tana Sackett, is that it offered the family a place to play. "We had club privileges," says Tana, "so I grew up on Oakland Hills in Michigan – a pretty nice course."

Tana went on to have an outstanding amateur career, and, also faced the decision of whether or not to take a shot at the pro tour. "But I never could quite beat all the amateurs," she says, "so I decided not to go for it."

As for Al, he may have declined to tour, he certainly didn't forget how to compete. The fact is that Al Mengert played in 27 major championships – eight Masters, nine Opens, and ten PGAs – by far the all-time record for a club pro. "And remember," says Al, "I was not an exempt player. I had to qualify every time." He's also especially proud of having won six Section PGA Championships in six different sections of the country, which no other pro in the history of the PGA has accomplished.

Since turning 70, Al has shot 64 twice – "two of the greatest rounds of my life." And if his score climbs at the same rate that the years pass, he'll remain content. "I just hope that when I'm 102 I can still beat my age by six strokes. I'll take a 96."

Acknowledgements

First of all, I want to thank Allan Stark, our publisher at Andrews/McMeel, for coming up with the idea for this book. To Michael Reagan, who offered me the marvelous opportunity to meet, photograph, and learn from all of the golfers who appear in the book, I want to say thank you for that vote of confidence. John Yow is owed every readers gratitude for crafting scattered thoughts from the interviews into cogent essays.

Without substantial efforts from a great number of people, this book could not have been produced, particularly not in the very short period of time that was available. No one was more vital to that effort than Ginni Galicinao, who with enormous imagination, diligence and warmth identified, located and made arrangements with the many people photographed and interviewed for the book.

A tremendous number of people guided us along the way with assistance, suggestions, and introductions, and to all of them we are forever grateful: Henry Adams, Andy Andersen, Susan Anton, Bob Ault, Michelle Baker, Joe Black, Carley Wilson Brown, Amy Caruso, Linda Casey, Rich Clarkson, Aleizha Batson, Notah Begay II, Lori Byers, Cal Brown, Kathy Bryant, Scott Carpenter, Holly Carruthers, Penny Circle, Walt Collins, Bob Combs, Bob Conroy, Elizabeth Crawford, Jeanne Davis, Andy Deshazo, Janet DiBella, Priscilla Drozd, Chuck Eade, Sharon Farmer, Kathy Fitzwater, President Gerald Ford, Laurel Frye, Laura Galiano, Greg Gagliardi, John Gart, Bob & Betty Gates, Doc Giffin, Bruce Glasco, Tim Greenwell, John Haines, Jennifer, Harlander, Sue Heard, Bill Hegberg, Scott Heideman, Dan Higgins, Todd Huizinga, Laurie Hunter, Scott Janess, Judy Janofsky, Rusty Jones, Stefan Kaelin, David Kelly, Virginia Keltner, Sharon Knudson, George Koconis, Liz Kraft, Marice Kunz, Mary Beth Lacy, Carol LaRue, Jeff Lester, Ralph Livingston, Steve Loy, Bruce Lucker, John Maltbie, Toby Manis, Reed McArthur, Rick McCutcheon, Drew McVey, Carl Mickelson, Chris Millard, Jane Moy, Deb Murphy, Jacqueline Nixon, Bev Norwood, Michelle McGann, Mary Norton, Merlin Olsen, Joanne Pelz, Giancarlo Peressuti, Charlie Raudenbush, David Remy, Mark Richeson, Pamela Ritchie, Ginna Roland, Doug Rohrbaugh, Tom Rooker, John Russell, Karen Russo, Glennie Ryan, Ellen Savage, Scott Sayers, Dave Schneider, Steve Sharpe, Elaine Skov, Lori Smith, Rob Stevens, Jim Steiner, John Story, Bonnie Taggert, Mimi Teschner, Isabelle Thompson, Mark Thorne, Scott Tolley, Greta Wagner, Matt Walters, Andrew Wittlieb, Joshua Wortley, and Kim Zimstowski.

To those who gave generously of their time and effort, but for a variety of reasons their photographs do not appear in these pages, I want to offer a special thanks and a heartfelt apology: Robert Cavanaugh, Joe Conroy, Bruce Edwards, Susan Henderson, Gus Robinson, and Jim Thompson.

And to Susan Drinker, my wife and partner, I owe thanks far beyond the reach of words. She is not only a guiding light in my creative endeavors but also the digital magician who, with her computer, brought an elegant polish to my photographs.